W9-ATE-648

MORE SALES, LESS TIME

ALSO BY JILL KONRATH

Agile Selling

SNAP Selling

Selling to Big Companies

MORE SALES, LESS TIME

SURPRISINGLY SIMPLE STRATEGIES FOR TODAY'S CRAZY-BUSY SELLERS

JILL KONRATH

PORTFOLIO/PENGUIN

An imprint of Penguin Random House LLC
375 Hudson Street
New York, New York 10014

Copyright © 2016 by Jill Konrath

Penguin supports copyright. Copyright fuels creativity, encourages diverse voices, promotes free speech, and creates a vibrant culture. Thank you for buying an authorized edition of this book and for complying with copyright laws by not reproducing, scanning, or distributing any part of it in any form without permission. You are supporting writers and allowing Penguin to continue to publish books for every reader.

Most Portfolio books are available at a discount when purchased in quantity for sales promotions or corporate use. Special editions, which include personalized covers, excerpts, and corporate imprints, can be created when purchased in large quantities. For more information, please call (212) 572-2232 or e-mail specialmarkets@penguinrandomhouse .com. Your local bookstore can also assist with discounted bulk purchases using the Penguin Random House corporate Business-to-Business program. For assistance in locating a participating retailer, e-mail B2B@penguinrandomhouse.com.

Photographs of the author by Media Junction

ISBN 9781591847267
Ebook ISBN 9780698155602

Printed in the United States of America
10 9 8 7 6 5 4 3 2 1

Book design by Daniel Lagin

While the author has made every effort to provide accurate telephone numbers, Internet addresses, and other contact information at the time of publication, neither the publisher nor the author assumes any responsibility for errors or for changes that occur after publication. Further, the publisher does not have any control over and does not assume any responsibility for author or third-party Web sites or their content.

May you enjoy the time of your life!

CONTENTS

INTRODUCTION   1

PART 1
ACCEPT THE CHALLENGE   9

1. A CRAZY-BUSY CONFESSION   11

2. AGE OF DISTRACTION   17

3. TIME FOR A CHANGE   23

KEY POINTS: ACCEPT THE CHALLENGE   29

PART 2
RECOVER LOST TIME   31

4. DISCOVER YOUR BASELINE   33

5. E-MAIL: OUR BIGGEST NEMESIS   38

6. IN-BOX DETOX   42

7. OVERCOME TIME-SUCKING TEMPTATIONS   46

8. MY WEEK OF DISTRACTION-FREE LIVING   51

9. GET BACK ON TRACK   56

10. TOTAL DIGITAL DECLUTTERING   59

KEY POINTS: RECOVER LOST TIME   62

PART 3
GET MORE DONE   65

11. FIND YOUR FOCUS   67

12. THE CHOPPING BLOCK   72

13. DESIGN A BETTER WAY   77

14. OPTIMIZE YOUR PLAN   83

15. GIVE ME A BREAK   88

16. QUICK-START STRATEGIES   93

17. OPEN AND CLOSE STRONG   98

KEY POINTS: GET MORE DONE   103

PART 4
MAKE IT EASIER   105

18. THE TIME MASTER   107

19. THE "AS IF" PHENOMENON   111

20. PATH OF LEAST RESISTANCE   115

21. GET INTO CHARACTER   119

TIME MASTER MANIFESTO   122

PART 5
ADD THE SECRET SAUCE 125

22. **WORK WORTH DOING** 127

23. **A REAL WAKE-UP CALL** 131

24. **GET YOUR OOMPH BACK** 136

25. **FIND SOME HELP** 140

26. **DO ABSOLUTELY NOTHING** 145

27. **WALKING IS WORK** 150

28. **SET UP FOR SUCCESS** 154

PART 6
ACCELERATE SALES 159

29. **TAP INTO TRIGGERS** 161

30. **DEVELOP TIME-SAVING SYSTEMS** 166

31. **UNCLOG YOUR PIPELINE** 172

32. **CREATE AN UPWARD SPIRAL** 178

33. **MAKE DECISIONS SIMPLER** 183

34. **GET BIGGER CLIENTS** 187

KEY POINTS: ACCELERATE SALES 192

PART 7
FINAL WORDS 195

35. **WRAPPING IT UP** 197

APPENDIX 1: **LEADING A HIGHLY PRODUCTIVE SALES TEAM**   201

APPENDIX 2: **KEEP ON LEARNING**   209

  TED Talks   209

  Videos   210

  Online Resources   211

  Featured Productivity Tools   212

APPENDIX 3: **BOOKS WORTH READING**   215

ACKNOWLEDGMENTS   219

NOTES   221

INDEX   233

BRING *MORE SALES, LESS TIME* TO YOUR SALES CONFERENCE   243

MORE SALES, LESS TIME

INTRODUCTION

SHORTLY AFTER I DELIVERED THE CLOSING KEYNOTE AT A BIG sales conference, Matt, a salesperson for a midsized software firm, approached me with a grim look on his face. "Do you have a second?" he asked hesitantly. "Sure," I answered. "What's up?"

That was all it took to open the floodgates. Matt started off saying he totally agreed with me that salespeople needed to be invaluable resources to their customers (the subject of my talk). I was glad to hear that. Then came the big *but*.

"But," he said, "I'm totally maxed out right now. I hustled like crazy last year to meet my quota. Then they went and raised it thirteen percent this year. I have no idea how I'm going to make my numbers. I'm up at the crack of dawn, working my you-know-what off all day long. On my way home, I pick up my youngest at day care. In the evening, I have family responsibilities. How in the world am I supposed to get everything done and learn our new CRM and do social selling and . . . ?" His list went on and on.

I recognized the pain of not having enough time in the day to do it all. It was my pain too. Likely it's something you're struggling with right now as well.

My response to Matt was empathetic but not one bit helpful. "I know exactly how you feel," I said, "but I'm not a productivity guru. I'm also having a tough time these days." Personally, I felt like time was taunting me: "Behind again? You'll never get it all done." I worked harder and longer hours, sacrificing my limited personal time to stay ahead of the game. Still, it wasn't sufficient. My work just kept expanding, demanding more of me. I could never seem to call it a day.

In my entire career, I'd never faced a sales problem of this magnitude.

While I—and Matt—dealt with this crisis of not having enough time, the entire sales field was doubling down on its obsession with sales productivity. Sales leaders wanted "more revenue per rep." Spurred on by big data, emerging software-as-a-service technologies, seamless integrations, and easy-to-use apps, sales teams were armed with the latest and greatest tools to sell even more—and handed quotas to match that supposed new capacity.

With all these productivity-enhancing tools, you'd think we would have been able to meet our quotas with time to spare. But precisely the opposite was happening. Virtually every seller I knew worked longer hours, yet according to CSO Insights, a whopping 45.4 percent still weren't making their numbers.

Matt's question to me—and my own recognition of what my life had become—made me curious. Why were we so overwhelmed? Shouldn't the development of all these technologies make it easier to get things done, not harder? What was I missing?

THE ULTIMATE CHALLENGE

For my entire career, I've relentlessly searched for fresh strategies to address emerging sales challenges. At Xerox, where I began my sales career and led sales teams, figuring out how to beat new competitors consumed me. When I sold technology, I obsessed over finding new ways to displace the status quo. When I ran a consulting firm, helping my clients jump-start their new-product sales was the ultimate challenge. Most recently, I've been writing, speaking, and doing workshops on the following:

- Setting up meetings with impossible-to-reach corporate decision makers (which I wrote about in my book *Selling to Big Companies*)
- More effective approaches for selling to crazy-busy buyers (I covered this topic in a follow-up book, *SNAP Selling*)
- Getting up to speed quickly in a new sales position (a skill I wrote about in depth in my last book, *Agile Selling*)

Never in my wildest dreams did I ever think I'd need to tackle the issue of sales productivity. In my mind, time management gurus were anal-retentive sorts who were preoccupied with streamlining processes and saving minutes. Being a sales snob, I was interested in more important things—like increasing sales effectiveness and driving revenue.

But at the time Matt asked me his question, I was sick and tired of being crazy busy. It was time to stop feeling sorry for myself and take action. With a vengeance, I threw myself into learning everything I could about time management and sales productivity. It was a problem begging for an answer.

I studied the work of neuroscientists, psychologists, time management gurus, cognitive behavioral specialists, psychiatrists, sleep researchers, and business innovators. Throughout the process, I kept trying to figure out, "How does this relate to sellers?"

Traditional time management strategies don't take into account the unique needs and challenges of salespeople. We have so many balls in the air—our prospect pipelines, long-term relationships, clients we're trying to close—and we need to pay attention to all of them if we're going to meet our goals. Plus, in many cases, we salespeople live on our computers. They're like appendages to us, necessary for our survival. Detaching from our devices, even for a short time, makes us nervous.

I decided to turn myself into a human guinea pig—to figure out how to stop fighting the clock and start winning again in my career. This book outlines my quest and all of the strategies and tools that I picked up or developed on that journey to becoming a more productive seller, with the ultimate aim of selling more in less time. It's my goal to help solve your problems with crazy busyness as well, without all of the hardship.

WHAT MATTERS MOST

To be successful in sales today, you can't just be productive. You need to be smart too: a good thinker, savvy, and insightful. Someone who brings value to prospects and clients with every single interaction. To do so, you need to be strategic, creative, and agile. You need to be up-to-date on what's happening in your field and with your prospects and clients.

The quality of our thinking is a huge differentiator in our work, yet few sellers realize just how important it truly is.

Our always-on, distraction-filled work life hurts the quality of our thinking. We have a harder time learning new things, prioritizing, analyzing situations, seeing new possibilities, and solving complex problems. When we bounce from task to task, that type of thinking is unavailable to us. We also make more mistakes.

Being productive isn't just about getting more done in less time—it's also about getting the *right things* done and doing them better. As sellers, we must free up time to ask crucial questions such as:

- What's the most important thing I can get done today?
- How can I have the greatest impact with this customer?
- What will it take to get multiple people to agree to move ahead?
- Is this the best next step? Would other options be more effective?
- How can I increase my closing ratio?
- Should I invest more time in this opportunity or not?

Answering questions like these requires quiet time and deep thinking. We can't determine the best route to take if we're frenetically checking our e-mail. The reality is we're not going to get that extra time we need unless we design a different way to work—every day, every week, every month.

DIGGING IN

I wrote this book for salespeople, account executives, entrepreneurs, consultants, sales support personnel, and business professionals. If you're responsible for bringing revenue into the company—and you're feeling overwhelmed—then you'll get value from reading this book and applying the strategies I share to your work life. My goal is to help you free up more time and do the work that gives you the highest payback.

Here's a snapshot of how this book is structured and what you'll learn:

In part 1, "Accept the Challenge," you'll discover what you're really up against when it comes to selling more in less time. This "age of distraction" is stealing our attention and destroying our ability to think clearly, creatively, and strategically.

In part 2, "Recover Lost Time," you'll find out how to save at least one hour a day by changing your relationship with e-mail and minimizing the endless, time-sucking distractions that you encounter, particularly online. You'll also find out how to recover when you invariably screw up.

In part 3, "Get More Done," you'll learn how to add another hour to your day. These strategies ensure your time is spent on what really matters, keeping mentally sharp and optimizing your schedule. For many, this requires a significant rethink of how you invest your time.

In part 4, "Make It Easier," you'll be amazed to see how a seemingly simple approach can virtually eliminate your resistance to adopting new habits. Within two weeks, you'll start seeing yourself in a whole new light.

In part 5, "Add the Secret Sauce," you'll discover numerous ways to keep yourself at the top of your sales game throughout the day. You'll be able to get more done, have better thinking, and get your oomph back.

In part 6, "Accelerate Sales," you'll read about key sales strategies that truly help you close deals faster that you can use alongside the other time management and productivity strategies I'll share in this book.

To help you make the most of *More Sales, Less Time*, I've included dozens of experiments you can do in a variety of different areas. I encourage you to become a scientist and run your own tests to find the best way *you* work. These experiments aren't meant to be hard work—they're meant to challenge and surprise you. When you add the element of fun to any project, not only do you stick with it longer, but your chances of succeeding also increase exponentially.

If you're a sales leader, sales productivity is likely high on your priority list. Right now, virtually everyone on your team is unintentionally frittering away at least one to two hours per day. I'd suggest you read this book together, perhaps a couple of chapters each week. Set up team challenges to motivate everyone to recapture lost time. When you do, your reps will make more calls, have more meetings, and close more deals. The best part is you won't need to hire more salespeople to make your numbers. I've included a special chapter for you in appendix I titled "Leading a Highly Productive Sales Team."

Personally, I think this is the most important book I've ever written—it addresses a universal problem from a salesperson's perspective. My hope is that for you, it's both sales enhancing and life changing.

PART 1
ACCEPT THE CHALLENGE

Crazy busy is a way of life for most sellers today. We have people to see, e-mails to write, calls to make, prospects to research, and proposals to prepare. With all this work to do, we definitely feel important, needed, and invaluable. But we also feel tired and overwhelmed.

Many of us wonder if it's even possible to get everything done. Truthfully, it probably isn't. We're tied to our devices, going nonstop from the moment we get up until we power down in the evening. We can't escape.

If we want to not just survive but thrive in our always-on world, we need to take a serious look at how we're actually working today. While it's often not pretty, it's always illuminating.

In this section, you'll discover the following:

- What happens when the digital world we live in collides with our very human limitations
- Fresh insights on changing habits and setting goals

Perhaps best of all, you'll discover that you're not alone. We're all overwhelmed and trying to find new ways of working. In this section, we'll start identifying solutions together.

GOAL: Understand the root causes
of our crazy-busy existence.

1.

A CRAZY-BUSY CONFESSION

EVERY TIME SOMEONE WOULD ASK ME, "HOW'S IT GOING?" I'D answer with a smile and a twinkle in my eye: "Crazy busy!" It was like I was wearing this as a badge of honor. In some perverse way, it made me feel important to say that.

While I might have fooled others that my life was great, I didn't fool myself. Underneath my chipper exterior, I was struggling.

In sheer frustration, one day I decided to record everything I did from sunup to sundown. I wanted to see my life as it actually was and perhaps find a way to improve it. I was tired of the "crazy" part being so accurate.

What I discovered was pretty ugly, but I'm sharing it with you anyway. Perhaps this day will even feel familiar to you. Here it is, a typical day in my life *before* I started my productivity makeover.

It's 7:15 on Thursday morning. Time to get up. I immediately head downstairs to feed the cat and make a pot of coffee. While it brews, I run upstairs, get dressed, and make myself presentable for the day. As soon as I'm done, I head back downstairs, pour myself a big cup of coffee, add a little cream, plop down at the kitchen table, and pick up my cell phone to start e-mail triage.

I quickly go through all the messages that came in overnight, deleting as many as I can, as quickly as humanly possible. It makes me happy to delete these messages—now I have fewer things to do for the day. I reward myself by playing a few games of Words with Friends. I then scan my favorite news feeds to catch up on world affairs.

After a half hour or so, it's time to get to work. I take my smoothie out of the refrigerator, refill my coffee, grab my phone, and head to my office, which overlooks the woods behind our house. This seventeen-second commute completed, I sit down at my desk and open my e-mail to read and respond to the messages I'd deemed important enough to save.

Before I know it, I'm sucked into an article from one of my newsletters: "107 Game-Changing Sales Statistics." There's a reference in it to some fascinating statistics, so I track the information to its source, opening that study in a new tab, which I save to read later.

Then I kick my own butt back to work, prepping for a project I'm doing with one of my clients. It's hard work, involving multiple interviews and customizing a program tailored specifically for their reps. I review my notes, immerse myself in their case studies, and start to think about how I'll structure the program.

As I do, I look outside and notice that it's getting overcast. I wonder if it'll rain later, so I open my weather app to check things out. Fortunately, the storms aren't rolling in until tonight. Okay, back to work.

Even as I try to get back to the project at hand, I start thinking about the meeting I have with a prospective client later this afternoon. It's a toughie. My prospect is really struggling to get everyone on board. It seems like all five people involved in the decision have totally different agendas. I ask myself, *What will it take for them to all agree?*

I head over to LinkedIn to learn more about the decision team. When I land on my LinkedIn home page, I'm greeted by a strategically placed promo for an e-book called *How I Leveraged LinkedIn to Close a $100,000 Deal.* Of course, I can't pass this up, so I click on the link, register for the e-book, download it, and then take a quick peek. *Good stuff,* I think. But I better get back to work.

Back on LinkedIn, I review the profiles of the stuck team members, taking notes on how I can create a connection with each of these individuals. I think about the best way to handle this conversation, the questions I want to ask, and the best possible outcome. I open a tab on my browser to review the company's website.

As I do, an alert pops up about a breaking news story. I click on it to learn more. While on the news site, I quickly scroll down to see if there are any updates about the presidential election. When no fresh articles pop to the top, another headline captures my attention: "You'll Never Believe What Kim Kardashian Is Wearing Now." Much as I hate myself for it, I can't resist clicking.

After a quick look (I'm not impressed!), I notice another headline below her photo: "Mother Cat Brings Her Kittens to Meet an Unlikely Old Friend." Within seconds, I find myself watching a heartwarming video of a big dog playing with the mother cat's two teeny kittens.

Oops! I still need to prep for that meeting I have later today. It's hard figuring out the best way to get everyone to reach a consensus. After a few minutes, when nothing good comes to mind, I remember a presentation I did for a similar client a few months ago. I open it up to check it out.

While reviewing that presentation, another thought pops into my head: *I wonder if Natalie has gotten back to me yet.* I open my e-mail for a quick check and see seven new messages. *I might as well read them all right now as long as I'm in my e-mail*, I think. I respond to all the messages requiring my input.

I finally close my e-mail to focus in on that upcoming meeting again. I stare blankly at that old presentation, still stuck. I wait a few more minutes for an epiphany to hit, but none emerges. When I look at the clock, I see that it's 11:45, so I head to the kitchen to heat up a bowl of soup for lunch. I bring my computer out to the table so I can brainstorm some more about that meeting while I eat. I jot down a few thoughts, some questions to ask, and an issue I want to bring up.

As I eat my soup, I remember that I forgot to congratulate Anthony, my new client, on his recent promotion. Back into e-mail I go to jot off a quick note. As I do, I see that another message has just arrived from Ravi, who's having a billing problem. Darn. *He's an important customer*, I think. I better take care of it now. I send off a message to my assistant. I also see an e-mail from CeCe. She has some questions regarding the recent proposal. Yup. I need to tackle that one now too if we want to close the deal this month.

Before I know it, it's time for my afternoon meeting. I head back to my office for the call, which lasts nearly an hour. It goes okay, but clearly it's going to be tough to reach a consensus on our direction. I'm smart enough not to fool myself about the likelihood of success. And I can't help but consider how much time I've already invested with this prospect. I briefly wonder if I could have done anything different to prepare for the meeting. When no new insight strikes, I decide to check e-mail instead.

I then take a quick look at my to-do list. Argh. There are a few prospects I need to connect with today; I can't put that off any longer. I dash off a few e-mails and make several follow-up calls. Thankfully, no one answers the phone, so I leave messages.

When I look at the clock again, it's 4:30. I need to contact a friend about a birthday party we're throwing together. I also want to check in on my mom, as she's been having some health issues.

Before I know it, the "official" workday is over—but I'm not done. I barely made a dent in the client project I started working on that morning. I don't know how I'm going to get it done. Seriously. Clearly, I'll have to dig in later tonight and try to make some progress. I don't have any choice, actually. It's what people pay me to deliver—and I don't disappoint them.

Except now I feel further behind than I did starting the day. After cooking my favorite chicken stir-fry recipe (which is quick to whip up) and having dinner with my husband, I drive to the grocery store. While waiting for the stoplight to turn green, I check my e-mails. At the store, I quickly stock up on the essentials. Then, as I wait impatiently in a long line to check out, I take a look at my e-mail again.

During the course of the evening, while watching a bit of TV and working on that project, I'm on and off e-mail a few more times. I manage to pull together an initial workshop outline but it still needs fleshing out. I play a couple more rounds in my Words with Friends game, hop onto Facebook to see what's happening there, pop over to Twitter to see if there's anything new I should be aware of—and check LinkedIn again too.

I then go upstairs and get ready for bed. Before I shut down for the night, I check e-mail one last time. Don't ask me why—I'm certainly not going to reply to anyone at that hour. Maybe I just like to end the evening deleting one last message from the next day's stack.

I feel like I'm a rat on a treadmill who's not allowed to stop. But that's how I've been working for the past few years.

I wouldn't be surprised if your day resembles what mine used to look like.

To find out if distractions are hurting your productivity, take this mini quiz.

DISTRACTION QUIZ

Mark an *X* on all those that apply to you. Be truthful!

☐ **1.** I keep checking to see if any new e-mail messages have arrived.

☐ **2.** I frequently bounce from one sales activity to the next (e-mails, research, phone calls, CRM updates, proposals, social media).

☐ **3.** Being "crazy busy" is exhilarating. I love, love, love it.

☐ **4.** Even if no one interrupts me, it's hard to stay focused on a task for more than half an hour.

☐ **5.** I sit at my desk staring at screens for long periods of time during the day.

☐ **6.** Thirty-plus minutes can easily disappear due to following interesting links.

☐ **7.** I'm under lots of pressure (self-imposed or management) to get results.

☐ **8.** My to-do list feels like it's never ending.

☐ **9.** I get irritable or bored when I can't check e-mail or go online.

☐ **10.** When working on something tough, I catch myself going online whenever I get stuck.

Count up your *X*s. If you only have one or two, you might be a bit distracted but doing fine. But if you've checked many boxes, it's increasingly hard for you to sell more in less time.

Before we get into tackling the many problems of working this way, however, we need to understand why we behave the way we do—and what factors, internal and external, contribute to this crazy busyness.

2.

AGE OF DISTRACTION

EVERY DAY THE CYCLE REPEATED ITSELF: UP EARLY, WORK straight through the day with lunch at my desk. On and off e-mail, in and out of LinkedIn, before stopping for dinner—and then back at it for another round before bedtime.

Working nonstop was exhausting, but I couldn't figure out how to get it all done if I didn't. And all that time wasn't adding up to phenomenal work either. I was losing my oomph. My focus was fragmented, my thinking second-rate. I had trouble starting new projects and finishing existing ones.

In frustration, I'd ask myself, *How could a reasonably productive, creative human being have deteriorated so badly in such a short time?*

I took solace knowing I wasn't alone. A recent Center for Creative Leadership study found that smartphone-carrying professionals (like salespeople) report they're interacting with work a whopping 13.5 hours every workday. When you add in weekends, they're working a total of 72 hours a week.

That's our life! We work more hours than ever, striving to reach our ever-increasing sales goals. Ironically, the very fact that we put in so many hours is actually one of our biggest problems. John Pencavel, Stanford economist, found that people's productivity dropped sharply after fifty hours per week and fell off the cliff after fifty-five hours.

All those extra hours we put in don't lead to better results. We're not actually getting more done. It's like we have this built-in work-o-meter that says, "I can handle fifty-five hours max. Any more and I'll slow down, putz, and dawdle. I'll look busy . . . but I won't get more done."

In fact, there's a good reason we can't do it all, despite our desires to the contrary. And when we come to realize how our bodies function, we can stop beating ourselves up for not getting everything done—and find ways to deal with these very human limitations.

WIRED FOR INSTANT GRATIFICATION

Sales today is a thinking profession. To be effective at it we need to research customers, search for trends, analyze data, extrapolate needs, solve complex problems, build consensus, develop strategies, and create new approaches. When we're doing this work, our brain's prefrontal cortex is running the show. This highly evolved, reflective part of our brain is the center of our deeper thinking. It's what makes us really good at sales and keeps us focused on doing what's most important.

When we're online, our amygdala—a very primitive part of our brain—can easily take over if we're not careful. Its role is to constantly scan the environment for stalking predators or any changes that might signify danger. From the amygdala's perspective, anything new that pops into its view is worthy of our undivided attention—at least momentarily.

Each time we spot something new, our brain rewards us with a shot of dopamine, a feel-good hormone. This dopamine surge is highly addictive, which is why we keep going back for more of any activity that gives us that high. In essence, we're wired for this instant gratification. We want to read that new e-mail or text message—now. We want to find answers to questions that pop into our heads—now. We have to click on the "Genius Wine-Opening Hacks You Haven't Seen Before" link—now, even though it never entered our mind until two seconds ago. Hooked again.

The cycle continues and we spend more time chasing dopamine-boosting links online, which prevents us from getting work done, stresses us out, limits our engagement with others, and, in general, adds nothing to our feelings of well-being. While it can be thrilling for a while, ultimately it's a recipe for burnout. As Nicholas Carr, author of *The Shallows: What the Internet Is Doing to Our Brains*, writes, "The net is designed to be an interruption system, a machine geared to dividing attention. We willingly accept the loss of concentration and focus, the division of our attention and the fragmentation of our thoughts in return for the wealth of compelling or at least diverting information we receive."

Is it any wonder that we're glued to our devices too? A recent Deloitte study showed that the average person looks at their smartphone forty-six times per day. That's nothing compared to the research conducted by Internet analyst Mary Meeker. She reported that people check their phones an average of twenty-three times a day for messaging, twenty-two times for a voice call, and eighteen times to get the time. We don't even realize that we're doing it. One minute we're working on something, the next we're checking our phone for no apparent reason. We sometimes don't even know how it got into our hands. Personally, I think we salespeople look at our phones more often than most professionals, hoping to find messages from our best prospects and existing customers.

HOW THEY HOOK US

What makes it worse is that we're easy prey for the savvy marketers and app designers who've mastered ways to commandeer our attention and steer it in their direction. They study what makes us tick and click, then feed us an endless stream of irresistible temptations.

In *Hooked: How to Build Habit-Forming Products*, Nir Eyal describes how companies hijack our brain and direct it their way. It all starts with a trigger, a cue that prompts us to take action with little or no conscious thought, like notifications, tweets, or "click to read" links. The companies want us to take action on this trigger. The easier they make it to open an app, push the Play button, or keep on scrolling, the more likely we'll succumb.

Once we act, we get a reward. Our natural one is a rush of dopamine. It could also be recognition, acceptance, the thrill of the hunt, or even mastery of a game or system. The best rewards are variable, meaning you don't get the goodies all the time. This in itself is incentive to keep playing. Finally, we're expected to make an investment, giving up something of value (e-mail, time, suggestions) in anticipation of future value.

The pull of these well-designed distractions is strong. It's really easy to be led into temptation when we're bored, tired, discouraged, or facing a tough challenge. Unless our guard is always up, this brain-hijacking cycle takes control of our day and impacts the quality of our work.

THE HUMAN SIDE OF SALES PRODUCTIVITY

Once we're hooked, we can't think straight—and we don't even realize it. Instead, we spend much of our day on superfluous, though intense, decision making. Every link and e-mail message requires us to stop, scan, and evaluate whether it's worthy of our attention.

The good news is we get better at this over time. But that doesn't mean it's good for us. We're all overtaxing our brains—even the digital natives who are significantly speedier than their older counterparts. When we're hooked, it's increasingly difficult to determine what's relevant or not. We have a harder time learning new information or skills. We're less inventive in our sales approach, repeating the same old strategies that give us the same old results. Even worse, we're constantly feeling overwhelmed, which prevents us from getting out of this destructive cycle.

Dr. Ned Hallowell, coauthor of *Driven to Distraction*, coined a phrase to describe what we're facing: attention deficit trait (ADT). Most people who have it feel rushed, distracted, and in a hurry, even when there's no need to be. They constantly hop from task to task, screen to screen, idea to idea. They have a tough time keeping their attention focused, even when they try. They feel guilty about not getting everything done but blame themselves for their inadequacies.

While not every seller struggles with these issues, many do. The onset of ADT is subtle and insidious too. It sneaks up on you gradually, until one day you feel like you're crazy busy all the time and you'll never catch up. Hallowell says, "I've witnessed the vaporization of attention, as if it were boiling away, while people tried valiantly to keep track of more data than even the most adept human brain could handle."

I knew exactly what he meant. It's how I felt every single day. I was doing my best to stay on top of my game but finding it increasingly difficult.

THE END OF TIME MANAGEMENT

Traditional time management strategies don't stand a chance in this built-for-distraction digital world. Most of them tell you to spend less time online. For a salesperson, that's not going to happen. E-mail dominates our working hours as we read, write, and send messages to existing or potential clients. It's nonstop, coming in at all hours of the day. Plus, we have to be online doing research and learning too. It's part of our job.

Yet the more time we spend in an environment that gives us quick hits of seemingly vital (but likely irrelevant) information, the harder it is for our brains to do the kind of creative and strategic thinking that is so necessary in sales today.

We need to stop being mindless consumers of content that keeps us occupied from dawn to dusk and clouds our best thinking. To regain control of our time and mind, we need to prevent our distraction-prone amygdala from running the show. Only then can we set up a way of working that will truly allow us to sell more in less time.

3.

TIME FOR A CHANGE

THE FIRST STEP TO STOPPING THIS CRAZY-BUSY MADNESS IS to recognize that the way you're working isn't serving your own best interest.

Changing isn't easy though. I'm not one of those profoundly disciplined people who can make a decision to change and then stick to it religiously. My willpower doesn't last very long—sometimes not even a full day. Telling myself, "Don't go online" or "No, you can't check e-mail" only makes me feel deprived. It becomes all I can think about. Before I know it, I'm back to my old ways, even though I know they're not serving me well.

In the past few years, my everyday habits had deteriorated to the point where they were running me ragged. Clearly I needed new, better ones. When I started my personal productivity makeover, I wasn't sure what those habits were quite yet; that would come later. My initial focus was on trying to figure out how in the world I was ever going to change since I'd been so resistant in the past.

As I studied habit formation, I found it ironic that my hyperdistractible brain also has a very rigid side that hates change of any sort. The basal ganglias' job is to constantly search for repetitive behavior patterns that can be systematized into a habit. Once the basal ganglia create the new habit, they go on cruise control, freeing up our brain to think about more important things. Charles Duhigg, author of *The Power of Habit*, states that 40 to 50 percent of what we do every day "feels" like a decision but is actually a habit. We think we're thinking, but actually, we're just doing what we've always done.

CHANGING OUR RAGING HABITS

To complicate matters, our basal ganglia rebel when we try to change. They don't like being forced to pay rapt attention to a process they've already systematized. They warn us that we're off track and raise alarms that we're likely to fail. They want us to go back to the "right way"— the way they're used to functioning. And the moment we stop paying attention, we default to that setting. That's why it's so challenging to integrate new behaviors into our life.

Doing things differently is hard work; we're going against our natural inclinations. It's even worse when we try to make a revolutionary change—like my annual resolution to lose fifteen pounds. Or my current desire to stop my crazy busyness.

I'm not the only one who struggles with this. Only 8 percent of people achieve their New Year's goals, according to John Norcross, a University of Scranton psychologist. His research showed that people who succeeded had an action plan. They invested time creating a system that made it easier to engage in their targeted behavior change. They also avoided situations that could entice them to revert to their previous ways. In other words, they ensured their short-term urges couldn't trump their long-term plans.

Speaking as one of the 92 percent who typically fail, I have to admit that my action plan was often nonexistent. Mostly I tried to drive change through sheer willpower alone, which I discovered was completely unsustainable. I also realized how hard it would be to keep on task since I was being fed a steady diet of appealing distractions every time I went online. In other words, I'd be virtually set up to fail from the outset. I didn't want that to happen.

According to psychologist Art Markman, author of *Smart Change*, another major reason I had trouble was that I focused primarily on "stopping" behaviors. I wanted to stop spending so much time on e-mails. I wanted to stop feeling so distracted. I wanted to stop being overwhelmed. Stop, stop, stop. That's all I could think about. It turns out that our brain needs positive actions to complete instead of more temptations to resist.

ONE STEP AT A TIME

Behavioral experts will tell you that when you want to change, you need to start with a goal—one that's specific enough to be measured. My goal was clear to me from the beginning: *I wanted to sell more in less time.* Initially, I didn't get more specific with that goal, because I was in a learning stage and I was okay with that.

Heidi Grant Halvorson, author of *Succeed: How We Can Reach Our Goals*, says that it's essential to ask ourselves, "Why is this important to me?" before tackling any initiative. Knowing "why" keeps us going when times get tough, which they invariably will. Personally, I wanted to spend more time with the important people in my life, have more fun, and work on some world-changing initiatives. Your "why" for wanting to sell more in less time is probably entirely different. You may be aiming for a promotion, a lifestyle upgrade, or more time with your kids.

You'd think a good "why" would be enough of a driving force to lead to everlasting change. It isn't—especially if you try to make too many changes too quickly, without a plan for success. That's why I was floundering. As I observed my own failures and got discouraged, I discovered the work of B. J. Fogg, a behavioral researcher from Stanford University. He says that many people don't even attempt to do things differently because the magnitude of the change seems just too overwhelming. That's why Fogg suggests implementing "tiny habits," which are simply the littlest possible step you can take to get moving in the right direction. Pretty soon, these changes worm their way into your life and you've changed with virtually no pain.

He's right. It helps to start small, taking positive actions and concrete steps that lead to achieving your overall goal. With each small success, you build your habit-changing muscles, enabling you to tackle bigger changes as you move forward.

It was obvious to me that I needed to tackle distractions first. They were killing me. My new goal was to reclaim one extra hour per day. If I could do that, I'd have breathing space. My plan was to do the following:

1. Immerse myself in distraction-prevention strategies and tools. I wanted to know what was working for other people.
2. Experiment with various approaches. Being a rigid disciplinarian doesn't work well for me. By staying open to discovering the impact of new ways, I'm much more likely to succeed—and have fun in the process.
3. Implement what worked best for me in increments, not in one fell swoop. Just one change at a time, so I wasn't overwhelmed.
4. Deal with the bumps in the road. I knew I'd screw up. I was prepared for it. I was ready to address setbacks because I refused to accept that I was incapable of adopting new habits.

It wasn't a complicated plan, but it was a workable one for getting started. After six months of step-by-step improvement, I wasn't so frazzled anymore. I was getting more work done and it was of higher quality. But I was still working too many hours.

LEVELING UP

It was time for the next step. I wanted a new goal that would challenge me for an extended period of time but not overwhelm me. I was ready to pick one that would make me gulp. I'd look at it and think, *What was I thinking?* It was an experiment designed to get me to look at my work differently. After serious deliberation, here's what I came up with:

> My goal this year is to maintain my income while working thirty-six hours per week.

Only thirty-six hours per week? Am I crazy? No—I'm inspired. I have enough revenue coming in but not enough time. From the moment I set that goal, something inside me changed. I could feel the wheels start turning in my brain. I could also feel decisions being made that I wasn't consciously making—like, *Well, I guess I won't be checking my news feed any longer.*

Also, I'm not persnickety about *when* I do the work. In today's world, it doesn't always matter. While meetings, phone calls, and workshops take place during the standard eight-to-five schedule, the rest of my work doesn't have to. What matters is that I try to stick to the thirty-six hours. If I can close more sales while working fewer hours, I'll be a winner.

YOUR TURN

What would it take to make you a winner? Clearly you'd like to make more sales in less time. But why? And what will you do to turn that into a reality?

Knowing your specific goal right now isn't essential, but think about it as you dig into the upcoming pages. As you read, highlight the ideas and strategies you'd like to implement. Take notes on approaches you'd like to try. Be willing to experiment.

Most importantly, don't try to transform yourself overnight. As an overachiever, you probably have that tendency, but honestly, it's a setup for failure. Instead, think in terms of steps you can take. Accomplish one, then move on to the next. Put together that action plan too. Remember, change is a process, and there are no miracle cures— there's only continuous improvement.

Hopefully by now, you're ready to get going. I'm excited for you to discover a world on the other side of crazy busy, a new way of working that enables you to be more successful working significantly fewer hours. It can be done.

KEY POINTS:
ACCEPT THE CHALLENGE

- For most sellers, crazy busy is a way of life and often a badge of honor. We're all under intense pressure to deliver better results in less time.
- Smartphone-carrying professionals report working a whopping 13.5 hours every day and a total of 72 hours a week.
- Working more than fifty-five hours per week has no positive impact on productivity, and actually has a negative impact. Past that magic number, more hours don't equate to getting more done.
- The amygdala (the primitive part of our brain) is constantly searching for new items in our environment, making us easy targets for digital distractions. Every time it finds one, dopamine (a pleasure-inducing hormone) is released.
- The more time we spend in an environment that gives us quick hits of seemingly vital (but likely irrelevant) information, the worse our brain gets at doing the creative and strategic thinking that's so necessary in sales today.
- People with attention deficit trait (ADT) feel rushed, distracted,

and in a hurry, even when there's no need to be. They feel guilty about not getting everything done but blame themselves for their inadequacies.

- Figuring out why you want to change is an essential first step. It gives you the motivation to keep at it when times get tough.
- The way we work is simply a collection of habits that we've acquired over time. To change, we need a step-by-step plan.
- Change is a process, not an overnight happening or a miracle. If you want to sell more in less time, it's worth it.

Download the Accept the Challenge PDF at www.jillkonrath.com/accept-challenge.

PART 2
RECOVER
LOST TIME

We live in the midst of endless distractions that beckon and seduce us. We're lured in by the gentle pings of new e-mails or texts arriving. Cleverly crafted headlines, creative graphics, and funny videos further entice us. We live in fear of missing out (FOMO), so we constantly check our multiple social media feeds.

As sellers, we can't escape these distractions either. We have to be online to do our jobs. We have to be in constant contact with our prospects and customers. We have to be up-to-date on business happenings. We have to meet our quotas.

To sell more in less time, it's imperative for us to regain control of the following:

- **Time:** We're bleeding time. It's oozing out of our day, far more than we realize. It's not uncommon for sellers to lose several hours a day on activities that provide minimal value.
- **Mind:** We're not plugging into our best thinking. Constant distractions prevent us from concentrating on tough challenges, coming up with fresh strategies, and getting in the flow on big projects.

Our first step is to get those lost hours back. Beginning anyplace else is a fool's errand.

GOAL: Rescue one to two hours each day.
Stop feeling frazzled.

PS: Please note that in this section I've featured a number of apps that can help you salvage your lost time. While the specific ones I reference may not be around forever, if they aren't, I'm sure they'll be replaced with even better ones.

4.

DISCOVER YOUR BASELINE

EVERY CHANGE INITIATIVE SHOULD BEGIN WITH A THOR- ough understanding of the starting point. We need to know exactly where we stand today—the good, the bad, and the downright ugly.

After recording what I did for a single day, I was pretty appalled. But I also realized that what I had was just a snapshot in time. I needed more data. On the advice of productivity experts, I decided to fill out a detailed time-tracking log, recording what I was doing in fifteen-minute increments. Experts recommend keeping this log for a month and then analyzing it to see how you're spending your time. You can then look for problem areas and focus on what you want to change.

It seemed simple enough. After finding a template online, I printed out multiple copies, ready to get started. The next morning, a clean log greeted me when I arrived in the kitchen. I dutifully recorded my prework routine. When I moved into my office to get going for the day, it wasn't long before I ran into trouble. Categorizing things like conference calls, proposal writing, or workshop prep was pretty straightforward. However, with my constant activity switching, it was impossible to get a clear picture of what I was doing even in those fifteen-minute segments.

For some people, time tracking works like a charm. I was a total failure at it. Keeping the log felt like a ball and chain around my neck. After a couple of days I quit, rationalizing that the exercise wasn't designed for sellers. Our job was simply too varied to make a month-long log an effective tool.

Excuses, excuses. Deep down, I now think I was trying to sabotage the project. I was fighting the truth—that I was my own worst enemy.

AN APP TO THE RESCUE

Just when I was ready to give up, I stumbled onto a productivity app called RescueTime. It tracks your digital life so you don't have to record your moment-by-moment behavior. At the end of the day, the program tells you how much time you spent on various applications (e.g., Word, e-mail, Excel, PowerPoint) as well as different websites.

RescueTime seemed like the answer to my prayers: I could ditch the daily log and let technology take over. I decided to invest in the premium version (it costs peanuts) so I could also track time away from the computer. That way I'd know how much time I spent on the phone, in meetings, in transit, and more. Additionally, I could set specific goals such as reducing time spent on various apps or on specific websites. Every day, I'd get a report on my progress.

The first week I used RescueTime, I worked the way I always did so I could get a realistic picture of my personal baseline. The results were atrocious. I was on the computer all day long, often wasting time, just like I described in the first chapter. No wonder I was drowning and distracted. That was the truth I didn't want to see. But now it was staring me in the face, blatantly obvious.

E-mail consumed over three hours of my day. That's how often I was in my mail app, checking for messages, writing them, or reading them. My usage was intermittent and continuous: three minutes here, ten minutes there most of the day. It all added up to a huge amount of time. Worse yet, I always felt like I couldn't keep up with it.

It was interesting data and eye-opening for sure. And I now knew my starting point.

OBSERVING YOURSELF

There's a curious phenomenon called the Hawthorne effect that happens when people start tracking behavior of any sort. While doing a productivity experiment, Harvard researchers discovered that human subjects change what they're doing simply because they're being studied. Often, performance improves. This occurs even when you record and evaluate your own behavior.

After that first week, I saw this happening firsthand. Just knowing that RescueTime was running in the background as a silent observer caused me to be more discerning in how I spent my time. When I did go off task with things like a quick Facebook check, I rebounded more quickly than I would have had I not been tracking my working hours.

At the end of each day, I'd check my stats to see how I'd spent my time. It was informative and inspired me to keep going. I started setting goals to reduce how much time I spent on my various online activities. Ultimately, I became a bit competitive with myself.

Over the next eight weeks, things slowly improved—until LinkedIn named me a "sales influencer." To drive more usage on their new smartphone app, they began suggesting to salespeople that they might want to "follow" me. In the first thirty-seven days (but who's count-ing?) after being named an influencer, my follower count jumped from 19,907 to 52,997.

Initially, I obsessed over the growing numbers. I tracked them hourly, sometimes even refreshing the screen every few seconds to see if there were any changes. I checked my "competitors" to see if their numbers were growing as rapidly as mine. I added more LinkedIn updates to my profile and spent time replying to people's comments.

I was definitely crazed. My RescueTime statistics tanked. Be-cause every LinkedIn check led me to click on new links, my behavior was even worse than when I'd started. Not wanting to look bad (even to myself), I went so far as to off-load this feverish checking to my phone. That finally stopped when I downloaded Moment, an app similar to RescueTime that would track smartphone usage. Ulti-mately I weaned myself from this continuous checking, but it took a while to regain my sanity.

Knowing my baseline was a wake-up call. Once you see how your time is really spent, you can't unsee it. Without RescueTime and Mo-ment, I could have continued to delude myself. It would have been so easy to say, "It's just my job; sales is crazy busy. There's no way I can do things differently."

But data changes everything. As Peter Drucker, legendary man-agement consultant, once said, "What gets measured gets improved." That's so true. With these two apps, I could now set goals, track my progress, and start cultivating a better way to work. Clearly, after ex-amining my reports, e-mail was my most addictive pleasure, taking up an inordinate amount of time each day. There had to be a better way to deal with it.

BASELINE EXPERIMENT

Download RescueTime or a similar time-tracking app for your computer. For your phone or tablet, use Moment or BreakFree. It doesn't take long to get them set up. Then, just do work the way you normally do, with no changes at all for a single day. The next morning, take a look at your stats. Ask yourself, "What can I learn from this snapshot in time? What changes might help me be more productive?"

Extend your experiment to a week—and then a month. Analyze the data to identify trends and personal pitfalls. Set improvement goals such as reducing time spent on e-mail or Facebook. Then, let these apps track your progress. BreakFree even gives you an "addiction score," which you can work on lowering.

5.

E-MAIL: OUR BIGGEST NEMESIS

I LOVE E-MAIL. IT'S MY LIFEBLOOD, MY CONNECTION WITH the business world. It's my primary tool for reaching out to prospects, communicating with clients, and keeping up-to-date on my industry. Unlike other digital platforms, I get to choose what arrives in my in-box. Yet at the same time, I hate e-mail. It's never ending, it's seductive, and it's a huge time eater. When I haven't checked it for a while, I get twitchy. Really twitchy. I feel like I'm missing something important.

You probably feel the same way. E-mail consumes a giant share of our working hours. We check it incessantly, hoping to hear back from that hot prospect whom we forecast to close this month. We sweat over the messages we're sending. While many of the e-mails that arrive in our in-box are essential to our work, a significant number are filled with time-killing distractions. In fact, a joint study by UC Irvine and the US Army found that people with e-mail access switched windows a whopping thirty-seven times per hour compared to only eighteen times for those without. Simply having our e-mail program available was all it took to entice us to check it repeatedly. With each look, we increased our chances of clicking on another link.

WORK INTERRUPTED

How often do you quickly check out a new message as soon as it shows up in your in-box? Sociologist Judy Wajcman, in an article titled "Constant Connectivity," reported that 70 percent of e-mails received are attended to within six seconds of their arrival in our in-box. That means we stop whatever else we're doing to take a look. Most of the time, the e-mail is not what we were hoping for. But that's what makes it even more addictive. Remember what we learned about habit formation? When rewards are delivered randomly, our cravings intensify.

We're just like the rats in the classic experiment conducted by Peter Milner and James Olds. Every time the rats pressed a certain lever in their cage, a small electric current was sent to a portion of their brain that releases dopamine when it's activated (which became known as the "pleasure center"). The rats kept coming back for more. In fact, those rats liked it so much that they did nothing else but press the lever to get their fix. They didn't eat. They didn't sleep. They just kept pushing that lever to get their dopamine, until they died of starvation and exhaustion.

Our brains are more similar to those rats' brains than we'd like to admit when it comes to pursuing dopamine hits. It's not just e-mail that lights up our pleasure centers. It's also accomplishments like responding to or deleting an e-mail, finishing a proposal, or finding a new prospect. Anytime we can check something off our to-do list, we get rewarded with more dopamine. Anticipation also fuels dopamine. That's why we keep pressing our own lever to check e-mail. But dopamine is also nondiscriminatory. It can't separate work-related e-mails from dangerously distracting ones. That's why we suddenly find ourselves on Facebook, BuzzFeed, or Reddit. Now we're bleeding even more of our precious time.

Jonathan Spira, information-overload expert and author of *Overload!*, says that his research shows that a person's recovery time from any interruption is ten to twenty times the length of the interruption. Let's extrapolate that and see what it might mean for you.

Say you check e-mail every ten minutes, six times per hour. Now, assuming each check takes thirty seconds, your *minimum* recovery time equates to three hundred seconds. That means it takes the next five minutes to fully get your head back into the task at hand. Even checking three times per hour means that you've lost fifteen minutes. That's 25 percent of your maximum productive time, or literally two hours per workday, that evaporates into thin air.

Once I realized all this, it was clear that things had to change. On one hand, like I said earlier, I love my e-mail. I also worried that I might miss something important. Plus, I wanted to be responsive to new and existing clients so people would know I wanted to work with them. But it was time for me (my higher-level thinking self) to be in charge, not my dopamine.

To edge myself into this change, I did a little experiment to find out just how many need-to-respond-immediately e-mails I received during the week. The answer was . . . (drumroll) . . . not a single one. My in-box was filled with client conversations, requests for information, newsletters, LinkedIn updates, personal stuff, and much more. But I didn't find a single e-mail where failure to respond within two hours would have cost me a customer.

Clearly, I had to stop deluding myself. In reality, I was wasting my prime working hours caught in a dopamine cycle. Yes, it felt good whenever a shot of it coursed through my system, but the cycle was definitely tied to my feeling constantly overwhelmed. It was time to take action.

URGENCY EXPERIMENT

One of the biggest reasons we check e-mail all the time is that we're worried we might miss a crucial message. For the next week, track how many e-mails you receive that absolutely required a response within ten minutes, thirty minutes, and one hour. See if you can extend the time between e-mail checks without impacting your business.

6.

IN-BOX DETOX

ONCE I REALIZED THAT I HAD MORE FLEXIBILITY IN HOW OF-
ten I checked my e-mail, I needed to figure out a way to wean myself
from my minute-by-minute obsession with it. I started by tackling
the "trigger," the cue that caused me to take action without any conscious thought.

For me, a little red circle with a number showed up every time I
received a new message. You may have pop-ups, banners, beeps, or
music to alert you. Every time I saw that a new message had arrived,
I fought the urge to check it out. To regain control, I decided to deactivate the e-mail notifications on my laptop. It helped some, but
being the sneaky person that I am (especially when trying to eliminate something I really don't want to give up), I found myself taking
little peeks on my phone throughout the day. That had to go too if I
wanted to be more productive. So no more e-mail notifications on my
cell phone.

Still, even these steps weren't quite enough to break my e-mail
habit. Every time I checked my in-box, I'd get sucked down another

rabbit hole as I clicked on the links in the messages. I decided to make it even tougher for myself to access e-mail. As an experiment, I decided to set some firm boundaries.

- I only checked e-mail at set times. Without them, my amygdala was running wild in my brain, screaming, "Check your e-mail. Check your e-mail." I couldn't concentrate. So I decided to do a quick morning triage to ensure I didn't miss anything urgent. Also, I decided to check e-mail at 10 a.m., noon, 3 p.m., and, of course, in the evenings.
- Every time I was done checking my new messages, I closed the e-mail program on my laptop.
- On my phone and tablet, I took a more drastic step. I moved the icon from the prime real estate on my home page into a folder on my second screen. By reducing the app's visibility and requiring a little extra work to get to it, I was less tempted to take action.

I quickly uncovered another issue that needed a resolution. Dozens of nonessential e-mails cluttered my in-box each day, screaming to be read or responded to. It was a continuing source of stress for me. I felt like I could never catch up.

Fortunately, I discovered SaneBox, a program that works almost anywhere you read your e-mail. You train it to filter out the unnecessary from the urgent. Today, all my newsletters and updates go into the SaneLater file so they don't interrupt my work. What a relief! I felt like I could breathe again, that I wasn't constantly behind.

Some of you may have set up rules in your e-mail system to take care of this. My friend Trish Bertuzzi has a rule that says if the e-mail has *unsubscribe* in it, it goes directly into her junk folder.

It also became very apparent to me that many e-mails came from companies from whom I'd downloaded an e-book or whose webinar I'd attended, perhaps even years ago, but with whom I had no other reason to be connected to daily. Others came from places I shopped, lifestyle sites, news feeds, charities, groups I belonged to, and so forth. I was also amazed at the sheer number of e-mail lists I'd been added to without actively subscribing.

That's where Unroll.me came to the rescue. It does two things I love: (1) sends me a daily digest of the newsletters I still want to read, and (2) unsubscribes me from those I want to get rid of. Each morning, when the digest arrives, there's a message at the top that says, "You have X new subscriptions in your inbox. Why not roll them up or unsubscribe?"

When I click on it, I get three choices for each newsletter. I can add it to my Rollup, unsubscribe, or keep it in my in-box. Some decisions are no-brainers. Others require thinking. I'm constantly asking, *Do I find value in reading this newsletter? Do I like reading it?*

Since I started using Unroll.me, I've unsubscribed from 1,037 e-mail newsletters. I shudder to think how much of my precious time was wasted reading content I didn't care about anymore or didn't want.

And it wasn't just about time. Every single e-mail requires you to make a series of decisions: Should you save it or delete it? How should you respond? Do you need to reply immediately—or can it wait? Who else needs to be involved?

The key is to reduce the number of decisions you have to make each day—even if it's just a miniscule decision like deleting a message. You're only allotted a certain amount of brainpower each day and you don't want to waste it on trivial matters.

As a seller, it's imperative to think clearly, creatively, and strategically. If you're in and out of e-mail dozens of times a day, you're constantly switching tasks. As you'll soon find out, this makes things even worse for us.

DETOX EXPERIMENT

We can't let our in-box run our life. Instead of reacting like lab rats, we need to check e-mail on our own schedule. Before your day begins, decide specifically when you'll check your messages. Schedule enough e-mail slots so that you won't be anxious between check-ins. Then, turn off the notifications on your primary device. Stick to your schedule, not allowing yourself to check e-mail until the allotted time.

At the end of your experiment, evaluate how it impacted your work: Did you get more done? Were you able to think better? If that goes well, try another day, then a full week. If it doesn't go well, analyze why. We can learn a lot from our failures.

7.

OVERCOME TIME-SUCKING TEMPTATIONS

I DON'T KNOW ANYONE IN SALES TODAY WHO CAN AFFORD TO get stupider. I certainly can't. Yet according to Glenn Wilson, adjunct professor at the University of Nevada, even thinking about multitasking causes a mental logjam. His research shows that just being in a situation where you can text and e-mail frequently knocks five points from a woman's IQ and fifteen points from a man's IQ.

Still, we do it all the time. Research by interruption scientist Gloria Mark shows that the average time people spend on a single task event—before being interrupted or switching work—is only three minutes and five seconds. When we work on devices (PCs, phones, tablets), we only pay attention for two minutes and eleven seconds.

What makes it even worse is that quite often we're creating our own interruptions, especially when we have tough things we're working on. Just the thought of making a difficult phone call and puzzling over what to say can create an irresistible need to check Facebook, right then and there. That's called "idleness aversion." We'd much rather be doing something than nothing (like thinking, which feels "idle").

With that in mind, we need to create barriers to the habit-forming hooks that websites and games use to lead us into temptation. Preferably they should require zero willpower since we can't count on having any when the urge hits us. Here's what works:

TAKE AWAY THE TRIGGERS

The first and most important step is to eliminate any external cues that invite you to leave what you're currently working on, even for just a few seconds. I turned off every single notification on my phone, computer, and tablet. No more sounds, pop-ups, vibrations, or anything.

What a difference it made! Yet very few smartphone users ever do this. Instead, they go through life being interrupted whenever anybody else wants their attention.

Some salespeople look at me with terror in their eyes when I suggest turning off notifications. Just the thought of not being immediately alerted to a new message gives them heart palpitations. My aim, however, is not to make you turn off these apps entirely but rather to check them on your own schedule.

Another way to reduce temptation is to close down apps like Word, Excel, or PowerPoint and your Internet browser or e-mail programs when you're done with them. Out of sight definitely helps these potential interrupters stay out of mind.

For a serial self-distractor like me, even disabling notifications and closing these programs still wasn't enough. So I started using Backdrop on my computer when I wanted to really concentrate. This program turns my screen into a blank canvas, totally eliminating my desktop clutter. Only the apps I'm currently working in are visible.

When I'm using Word, I select the Focus option under the View tab, which enables me to only see the documents I'm working on. I really do stay focused, then. (As I'm writing this, I'm using both these apps.)

MAKE IT TOUGH TO TAKE ACTION

In my experiments, I discovered that I'm far more likely to distract myself when I get stuck (if ideas or answers don't pop immediately into my head) or bored (when no task in front of me is urgent). When confronted with these feelings, I often check e-mail, click on other apps, or go online. Before I know it, thirty minutes have elapsed.

To prevent myself from doing this, I started using Freedom on both my computer and phone. This app blocks all my online time sucks (LinkedIn, Twitter, e-mail) for whatever time frame I designate. To get to them, I have to reboot my devices—which is a total pain, so I force myself to refocus on the work I need to get done. Even today, months after my first experiment with Freedom, I use it all the time.

Finally, I made it difficult to "accidentally" pick up my phone. When I wanted uninterrupted focus, I physically moved my phone to another room, where I'd have to go through the extra effort of getting up and retrieving it to use it. If you're in an office, stick it somewhere deep in your desk.

MANAGE THE REWARDS

Going online to distract myself was always a wonderful source of instant gratification. I found out new info about people in my network. I discovered fascinating articles, videos, and interviews. I kept up on world affairs. I didn't want to miss out on anything.

As a big-time "sucker for irrelevancy" who truly does love learning, I needed to keep the useful education separate from the mindless content. I use Feedly to aggregate blogs and publications I want to keep up on. Not only does it reduce incoming e-mail but it also allows me to quickly delete articles of no interest and even share the good ones via social media. Pocket, another program, lets me save all those articles that I've stumbled onto and read them at a later time, even if I'm offline. I still get my reward, but it just comes later, when it doesn't interrupt my prime working hours.

Sometimes I actually schedule time for my favorite distractions because I know that will prevent me from going to them on a whim. Taking a fifteen-minute Facebook or YouTube break can be a real treat after a period of intense focus. The key is to make these activities a reward, not a default, so you don't end up there when you should be prospecting or working on a proposal instead.

It's essential for us to stop the brain drain. We need all our smarts to do our jobs well. Constant task switching is killing our productivity too. Right now, we do it mindlessly. Awareness is the first step. Putting it into practice is next.

DENOTIFY EXPERIMENT

See what it's like to live in a world without endless notifications. Start by eliminating the alert from one single app. If you like the results, expand the experiment to more apps. Or begin by removing notifications from just one device or even just a few apps on that one device. Notice how reduced distractions impact your productivity, stress level, and the quality of your thinking. If you like the results, keep removing alerts till you're totally trigger-free.

ACCESS-DENIED EXPERIMENT

Download a trial of the Freedom app (or a similar blocking pro-gram) on just one device. Set up a work session where you're prevented from going online for fifteen minutes. Then extend it to thirty or sixty minutes so you can get more uninterrupted work done. Add extra devices once you familiarize yourself with this new way of working.

8.

MY WEEK OF DISTRACTION-FREE LIVING

AFTER USING MANY OF THESE STRATEGIES ON AN AD HOC, as-needed basis for several months, I still wasn't incorporating them all on a consistent basis. In other words, I was still being led into temptation much more than I should have been. That's when I decided to see if I could eliminate all distractions from my life for seven straight days.

I wanted to see what kind of difference it made for me. Would I feel differently? Would I get more done? Would I think more clearly? I was also unsure of my ability to see the experiment through. After all, I'd never been so disciplined before.

Over the course of one week, I committed to paying rapt attention to whatever task or project I was working on at the time. When I was on a conference call or talking to a colleague, I'd focus 100 percent on the conversation. I'd eliminate all distractions, even when I got bored or stuck. There would be zero multitasking for me.

It was definitely a challenge! But from what I know about human beings, when we're given a challenge, we rise to it.

PREPARATION

Before taking the plunge, I made sure I was ready. My alerts/notifications were already turned off on all my devices. There were no beeps, buzzes, pop-ups, or vibrations to disturb me. To keep me focused and on task, I'd make full use of all the apps and strategies I've already mentioned. Whatever I was working on would get my undivided attention.

It didn't take me long to realize I needed to make these adjustments if I was going to stay on task:

- Establish an e-mail time limit. Since it was so darned easy to get sucked into checking my e-mail, I needed to set a maximum allowable time. I decided that thirty minutes was sufficient for each of my checks. During the week, I set a timer and stuck to it. That forced me to deal with priority messages first, which I defined as anything related to bringing in revenue. I tackled the ones I didn't get to later in the day.
- Build in short periods of flex time. I needed ten to fifteen minutes of break time every few hours to read my newsletters, watch videos, and check out interesting articles. Otherwise, I felt deprived.
- Keep a notebook right by my work space. I was totally surprised at the number of random, distracting thoughts that kept popping into my mind throughout the day: *Send Chris an e-mail about the program title. Find out which software Jamie thinks is best. Make sure you ask Magda that question.* Normally, I'd take action immediately so I didn't forget, but with my commitment to no distractions, I had to write these thoughts down to deal with later.

With those measures in place, I got on with my week, eager to find out the difference it would make.

WHAT I DISCOVERED

Despite all my precautions, I still found myself wanting to create non-essential distractions. You read that right. I was creating distractions—all backed by a 100 percent justifiable reason (to me): I "had" to check e-mail to see if the signed contract had arrived. I "had" to go online to find a tidbit of information that really could have waited till later.

To keep myself in check, I reminded myself that it was only a one-week experiment. Just one week. I could survive that long. Fortunately, the distraction urges were temporary. But they would come back at intervals, most often when I was bored or stuck.

During the course of the week, I discovered other things about myself and what it was like to work distraction-free.

- I realized that I have magic powers. My phone could literally materialize in my hand when moments before it had been in the other room.
- It was *much* easier to get my tough work done. I'm talking about the kind that required strategic thinking, creativity, planning, and organization. I was definitely operating at a higher mental level than before, doing better work.
- Time flew by when I was immersed in my projects. When Freedom alerted me that my one hour of not visiting distracting sites was over, I was often surprised. Rather than leaving my work, I wanted to keep going. Often, I'd take a quick stretch break and then get right back at it.
- I got lots more done. I even found myself working ahead, on things that I initially thought I'd do the following week. In fact, I left my office early on several days because I was satisfied with what I'd accomplished. That was definitely a new feeling.

- When I talked to people, I was much more engaged in the conversation. It was more stimulating, livelier, and more fun. On the downside though, I was much more attuned to other people's multitasking—which felt incredibly rude.
- I felt less frantic and overwhelmed. Intellectually, I knew that when you're constantly multitasking, your body releases the stress hormone cortisol. But now that I was actually working distraction-free, I could feel the difference. I actually felt happier.

Another major thing I learned was that a distraction-free life was a utopian concept. Much as I'd hoped to cocoon myself, doing my work when it was scheduled, that turned out to be impossible. We sometimes have to interrupt ourselves to get things done, as I quickly discovered when my assistant told me she needed an article by day's end in order to send out my newsletter first thing the next morning. I'd forgotten to include it on my calendar. One of my prospects moved up my due date on a proposal, and I had to respond to that quickly. And for all of us, as well as me, sometimes kids, clients, and colleagues need attention now, not later.

It was a good experiment, definitely worth doing. I loved having the apps do the hard work for me. At the end of the day, when my willpower was virtually nonexistent, I found myself drifting into distraction. I couldn't have kept myself focused without tools like Freedom and Backdrop.

After the week was over, I kept using the tools, but not all the time. Part of me was rebelling against being so disciplined. But underneath it all, I think I missed the regular shots of dopamine that I got from my self-induced distractions. Before I knew it, I was slipping back into my old behavior patterns. Things weren't quite so bad as before, but the temptation was ever present, ready to lure me in before I even noticed. Clearly additional strategies were needed.

ONE-WEEK EXPERIMENT

Try going distraction-free for an entire week. To prep, turn off all your alerts and notifications. Get yourself set up with Freedom or a similar app. Use SaneBox or Unroll.me to manage your in-box. Establish times to check your e-mail. Build in some rewards. Then, go to work. As you're doing this experiment, notice how you feel and what you're learning while you're living a distraction-free life.

9.

GET BACK ON TRACK

I'VE OFTEN WISHED THAT I WERE LIKE MY FRIEND MARY. IN college, her term papers were done two weeks early. When working with clients, she's just as efficient. Nothing distracts her from getting her work done on time or sooner. She's as disciplined as they come.

Not me; I'm always getting distracted. That's why I've focused so much on prevention. But clearly I needed a backup plan for those times when I slipped up.

One strategy I found that works like a charm is to simply "push the Pause button" before taking action. Researchers at Columbia University found that if you postponed making a decision for just a fraction of a second, you made a better one. According to Kelly Mc-Gonigal, author of *The Willpower Instinct*, slowing your breathing down to four to six breaths per minute has the same effect.

In those few extra seconds created by the "pause," you can ask yourself if what you're about to do is the best use of your time right now. Should you click or not? Should you read it now or not? Should you switch tasks or not? Often, that's all you need to get back on track.

WOOP IT UP

Another effective strategy is the WOOP method, developed by Gabriele Oettingen, author of *Rethinking Positive Thinking*. It works really well for both minor and major distractions. In her research, Oettingen found that committing to a goal and creating an action plan to achieve it were important but insufficient. To get the best results, it was crucial to pre-identify likely obstacles you'd encounter and decide how you'd handle them *before* they occurred. Essentially, setting up rules so that "if X happens, I'll do Y."

These are the steps for the WOOP method that's helped countless people successfully deal with goal-derailing obstacles. You can see how I used it with my previously mentioned LinkedIn frenzy.

1. **Wish**: The first thing to do is to identify what you really want to happen. As I've already said, I was on a mission to sell more in less time.
2. **Outcome**: Next you need to articulate your "why." Personally, what motivated me was spending more time with the important people in my life, having more fun, and working on some world-changing initiatives.
3. **Obstacles**: Then you need to identify what can get in the way of achieving that. At this point, my endless LinkedIn checking was derailing all my productivity gains. It was a new obstacle I hadn't anticipated when I started.
4. **Plan**: Finally, you need to decide how you're going to overcome or circumvent the obstacle. I decided that the best thing for me was to use these strategies (note the if-then framework):

   If I get the urge to check my LinkedIn sales influencer status, then for one minute I will breathe slowly to let it pass. Often, this is enough to help me refocus.

If the craving doesn't go away, then I will get up immediately from my desk and take a short walk. Taking a bigger break allows me to regain my senses.

If I catch myself on LinkedIn when I shouldn't be, then I'll immediately turn on the Freedom app for one hour, selectively blocking the site. Much as I didn't want to be punitive, there were times I had to take this course of action.

Gradually I weaned myself down to checking LinkedIn once a day. Over time, even that became unnecessary—even boring.

As we struggle to achieve our new goals, we'll inevitably screw up. The key to our ultimate success is to think negatively and plan for the worst. Oettingen's research showed that only 16 percent of people do this naturally. We need to ask ourselves, *What could possibly go wrong, and if that happens, what will I do about it?*

This isn't being pessimistic. It's being realistic. We anticipate problems and prepare for them. When they ultimately occur, we're ready to take the best possible course of action. What's most important is that you are ready for the tough times. Either push the Pause button or WOOP it up!

WOOP EXPERIMENT

Pinpoint a single digital distraction that hurts your productivity but that you still succumb to. Put on your if-then thinking cap to identify different ways to handle the situation. Decide which alternatives would be most effective for you. Then WOOP it up for a week, fine-tuning your strategy as you learn more about how you react to it.

10.

TOTAL DIGITAL DECLUTTERING

DOING MY DISTRACTION-FREE CHALLENGE ALERTED ME TO other factors I hadn't previously considered about my work style. The cluttered desktops of my computer, tablet, and phone started to grate on me. Now, I'm not really a neatnik, so it was interesting to note how often they pulled my attention away from what I was working on.

It was at this point that I came across a study on visual distractions. Researchers at Princeton University discovered that the quality of a person's thinking was negatively impacted when objects in their field of vision were in disarray. Another study published in *Behaviour & Information Technology*, an academic journal, showed the same impact from a messy digital environment. In other words, every visible folder, app icon, open tab, or bookmark is another invitation to move off task—something I was trying to curtail.

I decided it was time to declutter the physical aspects of my life, too, starting with my phone. Over the years, I'd acquired quite a collection of apps for a zillion different uses. Their sheer number often overwhelmed me.

One by one, I went through each app, asking, Did it add value?

Did I like using it? Was it really worth keeping? I deleted dozens, easily. Some I hadn't used in ages, if at all. Others were near duplicates of my favorite apps and therefore totally unnecessary. It felt great to reduce the number of screens I needed to scroll through to find the ones I wanted.

After that, I focused on grouping like apps. I created folders for business, social media, reading, travel, lifestyle, and utilities and dragged my various apps into the groups in which they belonged. The only ones that didn't go into folders were the ones I used all the time—like Notes, Contacts, Clock, Google, Freedom, LinkedIn, MobileMe, and Settings. I wanted to make it easy for me to launch them with one tap.

I also wanted an icon-free home page on my phone. As I mentioned earlier, I removed my e-mail app from the dock at the bottom. It's buried in a folder on my second screen. The only ones on my home page today are Calendar, Phone, and Messages.

Finally, I prioritized my apps and folders. The ones I use frequently are on my first screen; lesser-used apps are farther in. The ones I'm trying hardest to not click on are buried deeper. I refuse to make it easy for me to get distracted. Once I redid my phone, I repeated the same process on my tablet.

Rethinking my computer desktop layout took a bit more consideration. I had about twenty folders beckoning me all the time. I opted to go down to three: WIP (Work in Process), New Book, and The Works (which includes everything else). Next, I tackled my dock bar on my computer, my browser extensions, and bookmarks. I deleted everything that wasn't used on a regular basis and was a potential distraction. Delete, delete, delete.

Finally, it's essential to figure out how to best manage our sales-specific apps. I had to think about the best way to most easily access my CRM and LinkedIn, as well as the various other tools I used for tracking, alerts, document management, and more.

It took me a couple of weeks to do all this digital decluttering. I actually took it on as an evening pleasure project (it had to be the dopamine!). Doing this decluttering required some thinking and prioritizing, which is always tough to do at the end of a long day. But because nothing I was doing was irreversible, there was no angst involved in my "playing" and doing a little experimenting.

Even now, months later, I'm still moving things around to find what works best for me. The truth is there's no right or wrong system. I recently started redoing my digital filing structure so that I can find the info I want with the least amount of effort possible. I've also become a bit anal retentive about my computer desktop. I like not being distracted by all those files lying around that seem to accumulate effortlessly. Often, when switching to a new task, I'll take a few seconds to put them in the correct folder so my desktop is restored to a clean slate.

Working and living in a digitally decluttered environment is less stressful. It prevents me from disappearing into irrelevant articles, low-priority projects, or enticing apps. My mind is clearer. I think better. I have more time.

DIGITAL DECLUTTERING EXPERIMENT

Set aside thirty minutes today to remove visible clutter from one of your devices. As you're working, think about how you might restructure your digital desktop so that it has zero power to distract you. Try different setups and don't worry if it doesn't look exactly like what I've recommended here. The best solution is the one that makes it easiest for *you* to get your work done. When you feel like one device is good and decluttered, move to another . . . and then another.

KEY POINTS:
RECOVER LOST TIME

CONSTANT DISTRACTIONS KILL PRODUCTIVITY AND NEGA-tively impact the quality of our thinking. As neuroscientist Daniel Levitin says, "Even though we think we're getting a lot done, ironically, multitasking makes us demonstrably less efficient." Use the strategies and tools highlighted in this section to rescue one to two hours per day.

- Download the free version of RescueTime. Discover how you're actually spending your time online.
- Track your smartphone usage with Moment or BreakFree. Find out how often and how long you're using your phone, as well as your most addictive apps.
- Deactivate e-mail notifications on your devices. Start with one and expand to others when you're ready.
- Check your e-mail at prescheduled times. Once you're used to it, extend the time in between checks.
- Limit the time spent on e-mail. Give yourself ten, twenty, or thirty

minutes but no more. You'll work faster and find you don't actually need to spend all that much time on e-mail either.

- Get SaneBox and Unroll.me to separate important business e-mails from other communications. Or set up rules in your e-mail program.
- Eliminate distraction triggers by shutting down notifications and alerts from your various programs and devices.
- Use Freedom to prevent you from going online when you need to get important work done.
- Use Backdrop to keep you focused on only those apps needed to do your work.
- Leverage Feedly and Pocket to aggregate and view interesting articles, videos, webinars, podcasts, images, and more—when it doesn't interrupt your schedule.
- Keep a notebook by your work space. Jot down ideas as they pop up to prevent you from acting on impulse.
- When hit with an urge that will take you off task, pause and breathe slowly for one minute until the need to break task recedes.
- Use the WOOP method to help you deal with common obstacles that derail your focus.
- Create an icon-free home page.
- Rearrange the apps on your phone. Delete those that are unneeded. Group related ones together.
- Bury your most distracting apps deep in your device. Put them in folders within folders several screens back and make them difficult to access.
- Clean up your computer filing system, dock, bookmarks, and browser extensions.

Each distraction buster takes less than ten minutes to implement. Start with one, get used to working in a new fashion, and then move to the next. And celebrate every distraction-elimination action you take. It is a big deal. Ultimately, you'll have more time to sell—and you'll be better at it.

Download the Recover Lost Time PDF at www.jillkonrath.com/recover-time.

PART 3
GET MORE DONE

The truth is we all have too much to do, much more than is possible to squeeze into a normal workweek even if we're not distracted. We also have competing priorities and are under intense pressure to meet our numbers. To succeed in sales, we need time to plan, research, prospect, engage clients, create proposals, give presentations, close deals, and handle tons of administrative stuff.

Certainly we need to get more done in less time. But more importantly, we need to get the right things done. Our focus should be on those activities that yield the highest possible return. As Henry David Thoreau once said, "It's not enough to be industrious; so are the ants. What are you industrious about?"

In this section you'll discover:

- How to focus on what matters most in your work. It's easy to get confused with everything we're juggling, but the truth is some activities contribute much more to sales success than others.
- Strategies to maximize your time. Once you've minimized distractions, the next step is to figure out how to best use the hours in your day to get more done—and to do better work.

This is all about optimization. Leveling up. Doing more important work—better—in less time. To make that a reality, it's essential to design a better way of working.

GOAL: Get the right work done—more efficiently.

11.

FIND YOUR FOCUS

IT'S FUNNY HOW, JUST WHEN YOU THINK YOU'VE ELIMINATED one problem, another one rears its ugly head. Until I'd minimized the distractions in my life, I had no idea just how cluttered my mind was. Neuroscientists are in agreement that the more things a person tries to remember, the slower their mental processing. Our brains get overtaxed if we use them as recall systems. Instead, we need to get everything out of our head and recorded on paper or digitally.

As I sat at my desk last January thinking about my upcoming months, I realized I had a very full plate in front of me. I needed to interview five regional sales VPs to prep for a half-day, fully customized workshop. The slides for my upcoming presentation in Barcelona were due. I needed to produce a thirteen-minute video for an upcoming sales summit. Six unfinished articles sat in my writing folder. It was time for a haircut. I needed to get back to a dozen different prospects, all at various stages of their decision-making process. I wanted to look for a new bedspread. A couple of really good ideas for new revenue streams were percolating in my head.

With all those ideas, tasks, and responsibilities vying for my attention, I decided it was time to put them all down on paper. By the time I finished writing, my list was several pages long. It was a setup for chaos and complexity. Not all items were of equal importance; some were work related, while others were personal. Completion time ranged from three minutes to many months for some projects.

Worse yet, I had no commitment to doing anything. Left to my own devices, I would likely gravitate toward doing the tasks with looming due dates since I couldn't ignore them any longer. Or I would tackle whatever was easiest so I could check it off my list. That's a lousy way to make decisions. It's also why the most important things never get done.

I got a big kick in the butt from Greg McKeown, author of *Essentialism*, who wrote, "If you don't prioritize your life, someone else will." That hit home. The truth is I was being far too reactive. If I truly wanted to sell more in less time, I needed to start looking at the choices I was making. Yes, I was busy—very busy—but perhaps not focused on what mattered most. I spent way too much time working at the edge of my deadlines, then getting panicky about making them. That's craziness.

Unless we live by design, we live by default. Whatever pops into our in-box gets our attention instead of what's really important to us. Our challenge is to learn to separate the important work from the urgent work. We need to stop confusing being busy with being productive.

In *The ONE Thing*, Gary Keller says that it's critical to continually ask this specific Focusing Question:

"What's the ONE Thing I can do (right now/this month), such that by doing it, everything else will be easier or unnecessary?"

That question is designed to make you think hard about how you're using your time. It can be difficult to nail this down because there are so many things that have to get done. We need to generate leads, handle customer issues, work on presentations, attend team meetings, keep our CRM updated, strategize on account growth, develop deep subject matter expertise, and more.

For most sellers, the ONE Thing is tied into prospecting or opportunity creation. There's no way we can sell more in less time without a decent pipeline. Even within prospecting, however, it's possible to further refine your ONE Thing by looking at what strategies provide your highest rate of return.

As I looked at my ridiculously long to-do list, I realized that my ONE Thing was writing. It creates more opportunities for me than anything else, plus it helps me establish credibility in the sales space with existing and potential clients. Yet it was often an afterthought, squeezed in after more urgent activities were done.

When I asked Jack Kosakowski, a sales guy for a marketing automation vendor, what his ONE Thing was, he said social media. He was laser focused on building a sales process that leveraged a variety of social channels to understand and connect with his buyers. Ultimately, this landed him at the top of his company's leaderboard.

Ryan K., an aviation insurance rep, named "niches" as his ONE Thing. He specialized in certain types of aircraft. Once he'd made that choice, he became actively involved in related online forums. He attended state chapter meetings for the associations his targeted clients belonged to. He networked with other salespeople who sold related services. It jump-started his career and provided him with a steady flow of new prospects.

Being busy simply doesn't cut it. We need to be busy doing the right things. The things that matter. Every. Single. Day. We can't let the tyranny of the urgent keep us from reaching our goals. We can't let nice, but not necessary, activities fill our calendars. We have quotas to meet. We need to practice ruthless prioritization—which sometimes feels like an impossibility when everything seems important.

What really matters though? Do salespeople have any common ONE Things? Ryan Fuller, CEO of VoloMetrix, says the answer is a definite yes—the more time we engage in selling-related activities, the better. Per his firm's research, top sellers spent 33 percent more time *with* customers per week, which typically equates to just two to four hours. But it's not just time that matters; it's the quality and depth of the interaction. Additionally, top sellers invested more time building relationships within their own company, making it easier for them to do their job.

Going back to my ungodly to-do list: it was good to get it out of my head, but I needed to be more ruthless in deciding where I was going to invest my time. That's a challenge we all face. It's time to stop being "spread too thin," so we can sell more in less time—and hopefully, with less effort.

FREE-YOUR-BRAIN EXPERIMENT

What do you have to or want to get done? Take thirty minutes today and write down everything you can think of, including personal and work-related items. Keep the list by you for the next couple of days, adding more thoughts and tasks as they pop into your mind. How does it feel to have it out of your head? (Note: you'll be using this list in the next chapter too!)

ONE-THING EXPERIMENT

Ask yourself Gary Keller's Focusing Question: "What's the ONE Thing I can do (right now/this month), such that by doing it, everything else will be easier or unnecessary?" Really think about your overarching ONE Thing. That may take a while to figure out. Also, on a weekly and daily basis, ask this same question: What's the ONE Thing I can do this week? What's the ONE Thing I can do today?

12.

THE CHOPPING BLOCK

STARING AT THE LONG LIST OF THINGS I COULD, SHOULD, AND needed to do, it was clear to me they'd never all get done. I took solace in the fact that my to-do list of 150 items was about average, according to the authors of *Willpower*, social psychologist Roy Baumeister and journalist John Tierney. But I also knew that the longer the list of tasks and goals, the less likely I was to get anything done.

As I worked on chopping my list down to a more manageable size, I discovered that these were my three essential categories where investing my time would have the highest payback.

1. PIPELINE

A few extra hours per week on these selling-related activities make all the difference in the world:

- Ensuring enough of the right opportunities. While lead generation, networking, and prospecting are often unloved tasks, they're also crucial to do. I definitely needed to spend more time here.

- Keeping decisions moving. Without constant attention, it's so easy for decisions to stall out—something I really hate. This is pretty common too. According to a CSO Insights report, 54 percent of the deals forecast by reps fail to close. Worse yet, a significant percentage stay with the status quo.

We also need to pay special attention to our top prospects and clients—the ones who if we close a deal with them can make or break our quarter. We should constantly be asking ourselves:

- What will it take to ensure they see the ROI?
- How can I make this decision easier?
- What can I do to keep things moving?
- Who else needs to be involved?
- How can I find new ways to be of value?

For these very important accounts, it's not enough to simply keep info on them in our CRM. We need to have them visible at all times. Recently, I asked three top sellers from different organizations how they kept themselves focused. All three listed their top prospects on a personal whiteboard right next to them, where they also recorded the deal value and next step. With this visibility, the salespeople kept laser focused on the accounts that truly mattered. Personally, I stick Post-it notes on my computer screen to remind me of my top prospects. I'm constantly changing things around as I get things done, new opportunities arise, or I close deals.

2. PLANNING

Time spent on research, prepping, and strategizing is equally as important as the time spent on customer-facing activities. Personally, planning has always been my saving grace—especially in the past few years when distractions have ruled and ruined my calendar. By strategically targeting the right organizations, preparing for conversations, and getting creative, I close more deals and better deals. Despite being in sales my entire career, I still invest time before every interaction to determine my objectives, conduct research, map out my plan, and figure out the questions to ask.

Despite the crucial importance of planning, it's where I see the biggest room for improvement for most sellers. Forrester Research reports that executives rate only 20 percent of salespeople as being prepared for the meeting and creating value. You only get one chance—and if you blow it, you don't get invited back. Thinking and prep time have maximum impact. We have better conversations, build stronger business cases, have greater credibility, and win more deals—faster.

3. PRODUCING

Like many of you, I'm an entrepreneur. We have to deliver on what we sell. This work is essential because it pays the bills. And if you're like me, doing the work is your favorite part of your job. However, you can't run a sustainable business if you neglect the selling and planning aspects of your job. Make sure you allot enough time to have a steady stream of customers. You'll also want to plan your "doing" work to capitalize on your most productive and creative time of day.

These were the priorities: pipeline, planning, and producing. To sell more in less time, I needed to stay focused during my workday on activities that fell under these three categories. Of course, there were other things I needed to do as well—tasks like database growth, marketing initiatives, updating contracts, and developing an online class. I would get to them, but being my new ruthless self, they were not going to get done until my most essential work was complete.

Chopping my to-do list down to a more manageable size was painful. Some things I wanted to cross off (like putting together a survey) were essential—even though I didn't like doing them. I eliminated some stalled-out prospects. I even whacked some items that had great potential but didn't get me excited. Starting a VP-of-sales mastermind group or a podcast series was never going to be one of my top priorities. Conversely, some not-so-obvious writing projects were saved from the trash heap because I knew they'd be good if I could complete them. I just needed to find a way to get started.

The hardest part was dealing with the items that were screaming for survival. "Pick me! Pick me!" an e-book concept cried out. I tossed it into my newly created Someday folder, a strategy recommended by David Allen, productivity guru and author of *Getting Things Done*. A pet project (creating free online sales training for small businesses) pleaded with me, "You've always wanted to do this. It's your legacy." I wasn't ready to let that one go, so I tossed that in the Someday folder too. I'd think about these items later when I had the time and energy. Right now, I look at this folder periodically. I'm fully cognizant that I may never get to the projects in it. That's okay. I don't want to lose the ideas. They may lead to something else. Or I'll toss them out when they no longer interest me.

As I looked at what was left on my significantly shorter to-do list, I felt a great sense of relief. Now it was time to turn what was left into a master task list of items I was committed to finishing in the upcoming week. On Sunday night I sat down and asked myself, *What's most essential to get done this week? What will have the biggest impact on reaching my goals? What can move my bigger projects along?*

Mentally, I compared and contrasted numerous options, forcing myself to make choices until I got down to the real short list: follow up with my top prospects, write a blog article, and prep for an upcoming workshop. Then, I took it one step further: If I could only get ONE Thing done this week, what would it be? The workshop prep won out.

I now had singular clarity about what mattered most. Of course, these weren't the only things that needed to get done, but they were the ones that would make the biggest difference. It was time to put my weekly plan together.

SUNDAY-NIGHT EXPERIMENT

Review your master task list of what needs to get done. Look at your week ahead to see how much of it is already booked up. Focus in on the primary things you need to get done this week and schedule them on your calendar. Literally block time out to do the work that you want to make progress on or complete. As your week goes on, assess how knowing exactly what you'll do in the day and week ahead impacted your productivity.

13.

DESIGN A BETTER WAY

IN SALES, SYSTEMS OUTPERFORM MIRACLES. WE CAN'T EX-pect to reduce our working hours and drive more revenue unless we get serious about how we spend our time. Minimizing distractions is a good start. Knowing key priorities is essential too. But they're still insufficient unless we have the right kind of plan in place.

For most of my life, I've been clueless that highly productive people think and act differently from me. They take their time seriously. If you looked at their weekly or daily calendar, it would be fully mapped out and optimized with activities to reach their objectives.

As a comparison, for much of my working life, my calendar was filled with lots of white space interspersed with scheduled meetings. While I fully intended to use that unslotted time to get important work done, it often never happened. Instead, I frittered it away reacting to other people's priorities. As Cal Newport, author of *Deep Work*, writes, "If you don't give your time a job, it will dissipate into a fog of distracted tinkering."

That was my situation exactly and probably yours too. There's no way we're going to meet our goals unless we spend time organizing time.

Highly productive sellers start their week on Sunday night. They take twenty to thirty minutes to review what's on their calendar for the week ahead. That's where we need to begin. Think about your ONE Thing, making sure you have time on your calendar for your priorities. Double-check that you have enough prospects in your pipeline. Figure out what you need to do to advance your existing opportunities. If you need planning time, put that on your calendar.

Then, use these strategies to power-pack your schedule.

WORK IN TIME BLOCKS

One of the most productive things you can do is to view your day as four to five work segments broken up by short breaks. Ask yourself, "What can I *realistically* get done in sixty to ninety minutes?"

In *The Way We're Working Isn't Working*, author Tony Schwartz suggests we need to work in sprints because this aligns with our naturally occurring body rhythms. Every hour and a half, our body enters a period of drowsiness where it's tougher to think and work. Trying to push through it makes no sense.

In that time frame you could call twenty prospects, put together a simple proposal, or plan for an upcoming meeting. You also have enough time to get in the flow, which means you'll be working at your optimal level. Occasionally, you may overestimate how much you can actually get done, so pay attention to what's really feasible.

GROUP SIMILAR ACTIVITIES

We want to avoid multitasking at all costs. According to the American Psychological Association, shifting between tasks can cost as much as 40% of a person's productive time. Multitasking also reduces our IQ. Here are some ways to group your work:

- Prospecting: Most sellers don't realize that prospecting is a series of very different activities: researching, planning, calling, e-mailing, and recording. You'll be much more productive if you separate this work into different time slots. For example, you might start with online research, jotting down relevant ideas, insight, and information. After that, set aside dedicated planning time where you craft your messaging. In the next block of time, make your calls. Finally, after they're all done, enter the info from your outreach into your CRM.
- Proposals: If you have to put together several proposals, do them one after the other. You'll get your mind in the proposal-writing mindset. This enables you to think at a higher level and do better work.

BUILD IN BUFFERS

Scheduling important meetings back-to-back is a recipe for disaster. If you've ever had to cut short a great meeting with a highly engaged prospect, you know what I mean: you spend the last few minutes of your conversation trying to figure out how to bring it to a close at the same time you're sending an e-mail to your next prospect, telling them you're running a few minutes late. Then, when you do get on the next call, you're flustered and don't perform at your best.

To prevent that common issue from happening, build in fifteen-minute buffers between meetings. Even if things do end on time, you have a few extra minutes to debrief and think about your next steps while the meeting is still fresh in your mind. As an added bonus, you have extra time to prep for your upcoming meeting, ensuring that goes well too.

Build in buffers when you're switching tasks too. Allow yourself time to finish thinking about one or slowly immerse yourself mentally in your next project.

LOOK AROUND YOU

If you're a field sales rep, one of the best ways to maximize your time is to plan your day around a physical location. Jeb Blount, author of *Fanatical Prospecting*, says, "The best salespeople map their territory by day. Then they plan their appointments and calls each day, within the grid, thus reducing drive time. The key is leveraging the CRM to run call lists by geography-based attributes."

Jana K., a multiyear top seller at a software company, is a master at this. She's on the road frequently, often sponsoring association meetings attended by her parochial- and private-school clients. Using her CRM's mapping tool, she can quickly identify clients and prospects in the same area as the upcoming event and set up times to meet with them. She is a master at maximizing her travel time.

Even if you don't have this capability, that's no excuse for not looking around. Your time is too valuable to waste. One of my clients is in the eyewear business. Their reps often drive a considerable distance to meet with opticians scattered across the country. Their top sellers set up meetings with other optical shops in towns along the way, ensuring the value of their trip.

SET A QUITTING TIME

If you feel overwhelmed, this sounds like an impossibility. If you work from home, your office (and work) is always beckoning. However, one of the smartest things you can do is say, "I'm out of here at [your time]"—and mean it. Literally at the magic hour, you shut things down and walk out.

Having a quitting time forces you to plan better. You'll be far less tolerant of any interruptions and distractions, even self-generated ones. I discovered that several years ago. My husband and I decided to spend a month in warm southern Utah to escape Minnesota's brutal winters. While there, I quit work every day at 2:30 so we could go out hiking. I got up a little earlier, but mostly I was just more efficient because I knew I had a stopping time.

Yes, there are times when you can't leave at the designated hour. You're in a meeting that's going on and on or you need to finish a proposal your prospect is expecting by the end of the day. There's a customer issue that must be resolved. Your boss needs to talk with you about your forecast.

Or, you may leave at quitting time but still have some work that needs to get done later. Many busy people incorporate a split schedule in order to accommodate other important things in their life—like kids, volunteer work, and fun. Having that quitting time is a great incentive to be more productive while also having a fuller life.

———————

Use these guidelines to create a system that works for you. Again, think system—something you do every single day because it works, a plan that gets you to the end result you want. According to motivation expert Heidi Grant Halvorson, goal achievement success rates go up 200 to 300 percent with the right kind of planning.

If you've never implemented a system to work by, it's a big change. But I can tell you this: I'm beginning to love a system, especially one that I've designed myself. Structure is freeing and systems work.

I-QUIT EXPERIMENT

First thing in the morning, decide exactly what time you'll be walking out of the office that day. Take a look at what's already on your calendar and what you have to get done. Dig in with a vengeance, making sure that what's most important gets completed. Make sure to protect yourself from unnecessary disruptions too. Fifteen minutes before your designated quitting time, review what you've completed, identify your next steps for tomorrow, congratulate yourself on a highly productive day, then leave.

14.

OPTIMIZE YOUR PLAN

AS I IMMERSED MYSELF IN DESIGNING MY WORK PLAN, NEW ideas jumped out at me from every direction. Some were research based; others came from people who were just trying to figure out how to get more done. As Russ Hearl, VP of sales at Datahug, once told me, "Don't assume that the way you're doing things is the best. It is simply what's evolved." If you want to level up, try out these strategies to see if they make a difference for you:

COLOR-CODE YOUR CALENDAR

If all your scheduled activities are in the same color, you're missing an opportunity to see how you're allocating your time. Recently, Juliana Crispo, founder of Startup Sales Bootcamp and a former top-performing salesperson, showed me her "traffic light" calendaring system:

- Green activities generate revenue. She codes any meetings (calls, demos, presentations) that involve customer interaction with this color.

- Yellow activities support revenue generation. They're what you need to do to have a fresh pipeline and keep deals moving forward.
- Red activities are functional, operational, or administrative—and not to be done during prime working hours.

With just a quick glance, Juliana can tell if her calendar is supporting her goals and, if not, make immediate adjustments.

THEME YOUR DAYS

When Melinda Emerson, author of *Become Your Own Boss in 12 Months*, told me that Monday was her writing day, I was shocked. That's all she did that day—write and edit—until her 4 p.m. staff meeting. Tuesday through Thursday were dedicated to sales meetings and conference calls. Friday was a catch-up day for unfinished projects. Because her days are scheduled thematically by activity focus, she always knows what to do and when to do it.

Jack Dorsey, CEO of both Square and Twitter, keeps ahead of the game by using theme days too. Mondays are for management; Tuesdays for product; Wednesdays for marketing, communications, and growth; Thursdays for developers and partnerships; and Fridays for culture and recruiting. With these themes, he develops a working cadence that keeps him focused on what really matters in his business.

We can do that in sales too. For example, Monday could be "prospecting prep" day, when you identify targeted companies, find out whom to contact, and do your research. Tuesday could be focused on outreach, initiating contact with the prospects you've identified. Wednesday and Friday could be days when you schedule as many of your "sales meetings" as possible. On Thursday, your main theme could be "follow up," when you write proposals, prepare presentations, or do demonstrations.

The beauty of day theming is that you know precisely what awaits you when you get to the office. You'll be mentally ready to work, filled with fresh ideas, ready to handle any challenges. If you get interrupted, which will inevitably happen, you know exactly what you need to get back to.

If you're also someone who has to deliver on the projects you sell, your work often requires a total immersion in your client's business. You conduct interviews, analyze processes, research competitors, and much more. Then, taking what you've learned, you need to create or customize something new. If that's how you operate, you might want to theme weeks instead of days. It can be hard to really get your mind into a project if the next day you have to move on to something new.

SCHEDULE LESS TIME

Leonard Bernstein, the American composer, is credited with saying, "Two things are necessary for great achievement: a plan and not quite enough time." As I pointed out, when we're under a deadline, we always work faster. A perfect example of this is when we're heading off to a vacation (if we ever decide to squeeze one in!). We can whiz through our e-mail in the days before we leave. Proposals get done in half the time. We quickly make decisions about issues we've been wrestling with for days.

For non-mission-critical work, I like to turn "less time" into a challenge. Specifically I'm talking about the administrative tasks that I consider a pain in the butt, that won't go away, and that absolutely have to get done. Rather than scheduling thirty minutes to do my e-mail, I'll give myself twenty minutes—or even ten minutes. Or I'll batch all my paperwork into a much shorter time segment than I'd allow if I were working at a leisurely pace. Playing this beat-the-clock game inspires me to get the work done. And I feel like a superhero for doing it.

Remember, the way you're working today has evolved over time, often without conscious thought. We can either plod onward, hoping for better results but not getting them, or take action to help us get done with our work sooner.

DECIDE YOUR DON'TS

The fewer decisions we need to make each day, the better. It frees up our mind to focus on more important things. Steve Jobs was famous for his black turtleneck and jeans. He didn't spend one second trying to decide what he'd wear every day. Instead, he saved his prodigious brainpower to focus on building great products and a world-class company.

Knowing your "don'ts" eliminates the agony of making one-off decisions every time you encounter a particular situation. Getting clear on this is a game changer, but it's never final. Every year I add more "don'ts" to my list:

- I don't answer phone calls from unfamiliar callers. I won't let strangers interrupt my day.
- I don't respond to RFPs. If I'm not in on the development of these documents, then they were written for someone else.
- I don't work with certain industries. How or what they sell is often too different from my expertise. They'd be much better off working with someone else.
- I don't do coaching or consulting. I'm on a mission to impact hundreds of thousands of people. Spending time working one-on-one prevents me from achieving my goal. Same thing with spending all my creative energy helping one company get better.

There's power and finality in telling people, "I don't." They won't come back to try to get you to change your mind. It also solidifies your conviction to focus on what really matters.

———

You can even create some ironclad rules to further simplify your life. With these rules, absolutely no thinking is necessary. One of my big rules is that I will not, under any circumstances, take red-eye specials when I fly. While I could get home sooner *and* save money, the next day I'm totally wiped out and grossly unproductive. I also have another iron rule about meetings: I always take notes. Always. If I don't, I'm virtually guaranteed to forget some important detail. I refuse to let that happen. The ramifications are too costly.

Get fussy with your time. Always look for ways to optimize and simplify it. But beware of turning yourself into a productivity robot. As you'll soon see, all work and no play is a recipe for disaster.

DAY-THEMING EXPERIMENT

Pick one day next week to focus 100 percent on a specific type of activity. Give it a name: for example, Monday—Prospecting Prep Day, or Wednesday—Pipeline Analysis Day. In the time leading up to this day, think about what you need to get done in order to optimize this theme focus. On the eve of your dedicated day, get everything ready to go so that you can start first thing in the morning. If you're prospecting, get your list assembled. If you're researching, identify what you want to find out. If you're analyzing, get the data ready to look at. When you get to work, get started right away.

15.

GIVE ME A BREAK

AS DILIGENTLY AS I WAS APPLYING MYSELF TO THIS NEW, highly productive lifestyle, after a while I realized I just wasn't enjoying myself. Yes, I was kicking out the work, but by the end of the day I was pooped. It was hard to stay focused on my key priorities. I felt like an efficient, fully optimized robot who was all work, no play. Clearly, I'd missed something important, but I had no idea what it was.

That's why I was fascinated when I came upon a study done by the Draugiem Group. They wanted to find out what their super-productive workers were doing differently from everyone else. Using DeskTime, a time-tracking productivity app, they discovered that the top 10 percent of their employees took more effective breaks. Specifically, they worked hard with "intense purpose" for fifty-two minutes, then took seventeen minutes completely off. Generally that time was spent walking, exercising, or socializing with coworkers.

Sprint. Break. Sprint. Break. That's what their whole day looked like. And more importantly, they never seemed stressed out.

Turns out, there's a reason for that. Like a muscle, our brain gets tired when it's overused, and we need to give it a rest. During its time off, our brain goes into task-negative (mind-wandering) mode. That's where it pulls together disparate ideas and thoughts, helping us come up with fresh approaches and break through mental blocks. Quite simply, we become more creative and smarter when we give our brains a break.

If you don't take a rest, your mind starts wandering away on its own. Before you know it, you'll be on Facebook, wondering how you got there. But it's just your brain telling you, "Enough is enough."

For today's quota-busting, numbers-driven sales organizations, taking breaks is virtual heresy, a frivolous waste of time. We over-achievers who work from home also hesitate to take time to renew ourselves. Instead, we load ourselves up with more caffeine or sugar-filled goodies to override our natural Pause button. Our body releases stress hormones to help us out, but that further clouds our thinking. Fewer good ideas come to mind. We can't find a way around our obstacles.

We're stuck in a vicious loop supported by an outdated attitude about time that's based on false information. Working nonstop does not help us get our work done sooner. It slows us down. In reality, breaks are not a luxury; they're a necessity. But not all breaks are created equal.

The absolute worst kinds of breaks—and the most common—are work related. Using your downtime to check e-mail or a social media site only exhausts you more. (That's what I was doing!) Talking with colleagues about a poorly executed new-product launch leads to more stress. Ruminating about a big deal that's in jeopardy only frustrates you more. Even quick, no-brainer chores like folding clothes or washing dishes don't help you bounce back either.

To recharge your brain, you need to do something you enjoy. Enjoy, as in taking pleasure from doing it and preferably non–work related. Was this ever hard for me to do! It just plain felt wrong to indulge myself in the middle of the day. But I decided to experiment with it and could immediately feel the impact of being refreshed. Here's what researchers recommend you do:

- Get up and move away from your desk. Walk around your office. Do some stretches. I have a set of strength-building exercises I use specifically at break time. Movement acts as a reset switch, releasing endorphins into your body that put you in a better mood. Additionally, your brain gets a fresh supply of oxygen, which enhances your thinking ability, problem-solving skills, and creativity.
- Assume a power pose. Harvard social psychologist Amy Cuddy uncovered a surprising connection between a person's body posture and their confidence levels. Her research centers on "power poses." Think of how Wonder Woman stands, how the big boss leans back in his chair with his feet on the desk, or how winning athletes raise their hands in triumph.

  According to Cuddy's research, when a person assumes those postures, it triggers a chemical reaction. Within two minutes, both men and women's bodies release more testosterone, a hormone that increases a person's pride, self-image, optimism, and aggressiveness. Concurrently, the amount of stress hormones in the bloodstream drops off, reducing fear levels. In short, faking confidence creates confidence.
- Be social. If you're in an office environment, chat with your colleagues. Better yet, plan a power hour with them where you each focus intently on your work for fifty-two minutes. When the time is up, you reward yourself with a fun chat. Meet people for lunch too. Don't eat at your desk alone. Being with other people is energizing.

  If you work from a home office, use your break to call a friend or your mother. I have a couple of workaholic friends who now rely on me to break up their days. I make sure to tell them at the onset that I've only got fifteen minutes. When we connect with others, we're more engaged in our work, we're more productive, and we get better results. Invest time in relationships.

- Play. If your company has Ping-Pong tables, foosball, or video games, enjoy the distraction, with a colleague if possible. Games refresh your thinking capacity and send you back to work at a higher level than when you stopped.

- Nap. If you're tired, take a nap. If you work at home, this is easy to do. It's a little harder at the office, although companies like Google, Cisco, and Procter & Gamble have recently added napping rooms. Even a short rest period increases productivity, amps creativity, sharpens mental acuity, and lifts your spirit. According to multiple Harvard studies, taking a thirty-minute nap in the afternoon restores your productivity to morning levels.

It's important to think about when you're taking breaks too. According to Professor Emily Hunter's research at Baylor, morning breaks deliver the best results. Hunter says, "We think we're like our cell phones, and we should deplete all the way to zero percent before we recharge back up. But we have to charge more frequently." By taking mid-morning breaks, "we're not allowing ourselves to get so depleted that we're at the point where we want to just get to the end of the day." In short, a morning break keeps us from getting more tired and distracted as the day wears on. But we can't forget to take afternoon ones too.

We need to learn to work with our natural rhythms, our on and off periods, not fight them like so many of us do. They're not afterthoughts. They're far too important for that. To work optimally, we need to take our breaks as seriously as we take our work.

Perhaps that's why I like this quote from *Atlantic* writer Derek Thompson so much: "Sometimes, productivity science seems like an organized conspiracy to justify laziness."

RECHARGING EXPERIMENT

For just one day, give yourself a seventeen-minute break every fifty-two minutes max. Do *not* use it to check e-mail or do any other work-related task. Instead, get up and move. Socialize with others. Do something enjoyable. When your time is up, get right back to work. Pay attention to how it impacts your productivity—and if you like it, do it again tomorrow.

16.

QUICK-START STRATEGIES

STARTING A NEW PROJECT OR NEW SALES ACTIVITY IS TOUGH.
Before we dig in, our brain automatically envisions the hardest part
of the project and all of the challenges that face us. To avoid dealing
with these undesirable things, it tries to simulate productive work by
diverting us to small, mindless tasks, like refreshing our LinkedIn
feed, checking our internal IM system, or filling out a form for human
resources. The longer we wait to begin, the harder it gets.

Before we know it, the work we need to get done has turned into
the elephant in the room. We can find a zillion reasons to justify our
procrastination. We delude ourselves into believing that we perform
better under pressure. We beat ourselves up for our lack of willpower
and motivation but can't seem to get beyond it.

The truth is we simply need to start quickly so that stress doesn't
cloud our judgment and compromise our work.

Once we get going, the Zeigarnik effect kicks in. In her research,
psychologist Bluma Zeigarnik discovered that when people complete
tasks, they quickly forget them. But if a person's work is interrupted

and they're not allowed to finish, the task nags at them relentlessly. Our brain won't let us off the hook until we're done. That's why mastering the art of the start is so crucial.

However, not every task can be completed once you've started. You may need other people's input. Resources may be unavailable. The sheer size of the project could take months to complete. To prevent the Zeigarnik effect from repeatedly harassing you, put together a plan for completion. That's all it takes for your brain to relax. Then it knows you're going to complete the project (or at least the next portion of it) in the near future—or even on a specific date.

PLAY THE POMODORO

To jump-start my work on new projects, I love the Pomodoro Technique. Developed by Francesco Cirillo, its primary objective is to get us started on nonfavorite tasks (e.g., prospecting) or ones that require deep concentration and quality thinking (e.g., winning in a highly competitive situation).

Normally, we'd putz around for a while, trying to ease our way into our work or hoping that something more urgent would pop up. The Pomodoro method gets you cranking it out right away. It helps you learn how to work with time, not against it. Hours don't evaporate into thin air. Instead, you end up feeling great accomplishment. All you need to get going is a kitchen timer (Cirillo's original timer was in the shape of a red tomato—a "pomodoro" in Italian) or the free Pomodoro One app.

Starting is deceptively simple.

1. Choose a task to work on.
2. Write it down on your activity log.
3. Set the timer for twenty-five minutes.

4. Begin working on your task.

5. When the timer goes off, stop immediately.

6. Take a five-minute break.

That's it. On your break, disconnect from work. Walk around, talk to people, get a glass of water, or do some quickie exercises. During your time off, your brain refreshes itself. It also lets go of its intense focus on the task, which enables it to make connections to other ideas, thoughts, strategies, or issues that could be helpful. Plus, the Zeigarnik effect won't be haunting you because it knows you'll soon be back at work; that's part of the plan.

Once your break is over, start a new Pomodoro session. Do this up to four times in a row. After the fourth Pomodoro, it's time for a longer break of fifteen to thirty minutes. Also, should you get done with your task early, keep working, picking up another project until the timer rings.

The goal of a Pomodoro session is progress, not completion. You're training your brain to work in these twenty-five-minute sprints, then taking time to reenergize yourself so you can do it again. That's how new, better work habits are established.

Tracking what you got done during each Pomodoro is valuable too. As humans, we're wired to make progress. Teresa Amabile and Steven Kramer, coauthors of *The Progress Principle*, studied 238 knowledge workers whose jobs all required creative productivity (today's seller fits in that category). On these workers' self-described "best days," they made progress toward their goals. Even small steps forward produced a surge of well-being. That's why it's so essential to track what we've accomplished. You can do it manually as shown in the following table. Or you might want to try out the I Done This app. Both help you feel good about your accomplishments.

MISSION ACCOMPLISHED		
Date	What You Worked On	# of Pomodoros
1/5	Identify 20 targeted companies	xx
1/6	Determine 3–5 contacts/accounts	xxx

Doing four to five Pomodoro sessions a day can have a dramatic improvement on how much work you get done. Instead of saying, "Argh, those two hours slipped by and I barely made any progress," you'll be saying, "Wow. I can't believe how much I got done."

SUPERSIZED PROJECTS

Sometimes, when the job we're tackling is complex or unfamiliar, we become easily overwhelmed. Or there's so much to do, we can't figure out what we should be tackling. Matthew Kimberley, partner in Book Yourself Solid Worldwide, makes a great point when he says, "Overwhelm is a result not of having too much to do, but of not knowing what to do next."

To avoid these bottlenecks, break big activities down into doable segments. For example, if you're planning for a big meeting with an important prospect, you might want to allocate your day as follows:

- 60 minutes: Review info about company, strategic initiatives, financials, markets; research key decision makers who'll be attending.

- 60 minutes: Discuss strategy with team members.
- 90 minutes: Put together presentation that highlights the business case for making a change.
- 60 minutes: Review and improve presentation.
- 90 minutes: Practice delivery and build in engagement.

As soon as you've mapped it out, put it on your calendar. You want to make sure to plan enough time to be fully prepared.

Breaking these big projects down into actionable chunks enables you to get started. The Pomodoro Technique throws you right into the work and challenges you to get it done with dedicated, focused attention. You'll build momentum, get work done faster, and do it better, which is crucial for sales success.

POMODORO EXPERIMENT

You have to experience a Pomodoro session in order to understand its value. Take a look at your master task list right now. What ONE Thing are you stalling on that you really need to kick into gear? Write it down. Now, take a couple of minutes to get your work space set up for a dedicated sprint to accomplish wonders in just twenty-five minutes.

When you're ready, set your timer and dig in. As soon as the timer goes off, stop, take a mini break, and then ask yourself these questions: Am I satisfied with what I accomplished? What did I learn? Am I motivated to continue this work?

17.

OPEN AND CLOSE STRONG

AS A BUSY PARENT, I COULDN'T WAIT TO MOVE TO A HOME office. For years, my mornings had been filled with trying to get two kids off to school or day care without forgetting anything. Then there was that forty-five-minute drive across town to the office in bumper-to-bumper traffic in good weather and up to two hours during our Minnesota winters.

You can't imagine my shock when I started working from home and discovered that I actually missed the drive. Alone with myself on my drive to work, I had planned my days and strategized about accounts. On the commute home, I debriefed sales calls, determined my next steps, and thought about what I had learned. But as soon as I moved home, things changed. I was at my desk in seventeen seconds— and not mentally ready for work. At the end of the day, I was hustling to make dinner or to take a child to basketball practice. There was no time for any reflection.

At that time, I didn't understand the importance of good morning and end-of-day routines. Instead I settled into a less-than-ideal one because I didn't know any better.

After reading *What the Most Successful People Do before Breakfast*, I knew it was time to rethink what I was doing. According to author Laura Vanderkam, high achievers have morning routines that start much earlier than you'd expect. They're often up at the crack of dawn to nurture their careers, their relationships, and themselves. By the time these top performers get to their desks, they're ahead of most of us and primed for the day.

I was jealous of these early birds. My thinking is foggy in the early morning. When I do have to get up early, it takes all my effort to kick my brain into gear, to get the creative juices flowing, and even to have intelligent conversations.

Fortunately, I discovered that being up in the wee hours is not essential for getting lots done. According to Dan Ariely, behavioral economist and author of *Predictably Irrational*, we have two to two and a half hours of peak productivity every day. He says that "if you get up at 7 am, you'll be most productive from around 8-10:30." Other researchers say that our brain is sharpest starting two and a half to four hours after waking up.

Clearly we need to create good habits around our morning hours if we're going to maximize our time. Again, I'm talking habits. Something we do every day because that's how we get ourselves in the right mind-set to do our best work.

FIRST TEN MINUTES

Once we get into the office, we need a good ten-minute routine to kick off our work. It has to be one that gets us focusing on the right stuff, right away. It helps to sit quietly at first, doing nothing—for just a minute or two. If you grab a cup of coffee, enjoy the aroma and let that become a signal to your brain that you're ready to start.

Then, rather than hopping onto a device, think about where you stand with regard to reaching your goals and what you need to get done for the day, focusing on what's most important. Hopefully, you've jotted some notes down from the previous day regarding what to tackle first. If not, decide what these priorities are. Then, review your calendar to see if anything needs changing or if more prep work is needed for upcoming meetings.

PEAK HOURS

Kicking off your day with a top priority is essential but often tough. One of the best ways to prime the mental pump is to first tackle a task that gives you a quick win. You need to do it. It won't take long, and when it's done, you'll be glad.

Just this morning, I quickly wrote up a description of a new keynote I'm giving to a group of entrepreneurs. My client needed it by the end of the day so they could publicize the event in their newsletter. I got it done early and it felt really great. Having it off my to-do list allowed me to concentrate on my top priority.

If you have multiple things that need to get done, follow the advice of Mark Twain, who once said, "Eat a live frog first thing in the morning, and nothing worse will happen to you all day." For many sellers, that live frog is prospecting, making the calls. Imagine if you could get twenty of them done before 10:30. Would that make your day?

Our willpower is at its strongest in the morning hours. You have the capability to make yourself do dreaded activities at that time of the day. If you don't do them then, there's a high likelihood that you'll keep putting them off—a reality that Brian Tracy tackles in his book on this subject, *Eat That Frog!* I can vouch for that. I've managed to put off some live frogs for weeks. Unfortunately, that only makes me miserable. I now force myself to eat these frogs for breakfast—and I've discovered they don't taste nearly as bad as they look.

Here are a couple more thoughts on how to get the most from your morning routine:

- Take a few minutes to socialize with your coworkers. We work better when we feel like we're part of the team. Efficiency isn't everything.
- Do something that gets you in a good mood. Look at photos of a recent vacation or favorite friend. Compliment a colleague. Smile at people around you. When you're happy, you're more productive.

Whatever you do, protect these peak hours at all costs. People will try to steal them from you. Or, without a plan, our default setting of distraction will take over.

FINAL FIFTEEN MINUTES

How you end the day is just as important as how you start it. You need a closing-down ritual, something that you'll do every single day because it's how you work. Rather than just shut your computer off and head out, take time to think about what you did today and what still needs to be accomplished. Review your calendar for tomorrow so you know what's ahead. Then, write down the three most important things you want to accomplish next.

By doing this status check the night before, you activate your brain to start thinking about these things. It will operate in the background all night long, searching for relevant ideas or information that can help you out. If you're stumped about something, pose a question to yourself. Again, without you actively thinking about this, your brain will engage in problem solving.

Another critical but seldom-used wind-down strategy is reflection. Take ten to fifteen minutes to think about and jot down what you learned, your accomplishments, and the progress you made. I used this strategy daily as I was working to change my habits and adapt to new, more productive ways of working. It gave me invaluable insights that allowed me to fine-tune how I worked.

According to a recent study by Harvard Business School professor Francesca Gino, reflecting for even a short time increases new-hire job performance by 28 percent. Executive coach Chris Holmberg insists that his clients reflect for a full hour at the end of the week. He says, "Startup leaders can't afford to have low learning efficiency. They must milk each experience for maximum learning. Reflection is the key for accelerating your learning curve."

To finalize your end-of-day routine, straighten up your work space. When you come into your office, you don't want any visual distractions to keep you from doing your most important work. Close down extra apps on your computer, leaving open only the ones you'll need for your first working session. Sometimes, I even stick a Post-it note to my screen to make it virtually impossible to overlook this singular task.

Having rock-solid morning and evening routines drives increased productivity at work.

OPENER/CLOSER EXPERIMENT

Think of one little thing you'd like to change in your morning or end-of-day routine. Make it small so it barely takes any extra time. Perhaps you can focus on your first five minutes at your desk. Ask yourself, "What can I do to help me jump-start my day?" Brainstorm some ideas, then pick one you want to implement for just one week, to see what difference it makes. At the end of each day, reflect on how it impacted you.

KEY POINTS:
GET MORE DONE

AFTER MINIMIZING DISTRACTIONS, THE MOST IMPORTANT thing you can do is to optimize the time you have. If you do what's most important to your success, do it right, and do it early, you will get the highest return on your time investment. These strategies will give you an additional one to two hours per day.

- Practice ruthless prioritization. To determine what to focus on, use Gary Keller's Focusing Question: "What's the ONE Thing I can do (right now/this month), such that by doing it, everything else will be easier or unnecessary?"
- Invest the bulk of your time in customer-facing activities or preparing for them.
- Keep an eye on your pipeline. Make sure you have enough of the right prospects—and that you keep decisions moving.
- Turn your to-do list into a master task list, moving unimportant or nonurgent items to a Someday folder.
- Schedule time on your calendar to do what's most important.

Everything that's important should be on there—or else you won't get to it.

- Spend Sunday night reviewing the critical tasks ahead of you. Get a jump start on your week by plotting it out before it begins.
- Work in time blocks. Ask yourself, "What can I realistically get done in sixty to ninety minutes?" For maximum productivity, group similar activities together.
- Schedule e-mail checks at certain times. Avoid the massive disruption caused by constantly visiting your in-box.
- Build in buffers. Between calls and meetings, spend time thinking and reflecting about what you learned as well as prepping for the next one.
- To optimize your plan, color-code your calendar. Make how you're spending your time visible. Theme your days to maximize your flow.
- Make fewer decisions. Know what you won't do. Make ironclad rules that you'll always follow.
- Take regular breaks. Never work longer than ninety minutes at a time. Then take at least fifteen minutes off to recharge yourself.
- Use the Pomodoro Technique to jump-start your work if you're finding it especially tough to get going.
- Develop a morning routine to get your day off to a quick start and an evening routine to close strong.

You have the power and the capability to design a better way to work. Don't live by default. Optimize, optimize, optimize.

Download the Get More Done PDF at
www.jillkonrath.com/get-more-done.

PART 4
MAKE IT EASIER

The best solutions are often the simplest. But finding them takes time. You have to immerse yourself in the details, integrate them into how you work—and then, and only then, are you able to discover a much more elegant way to accomplish your task.

In this section, you'll discover a higher-level mind-set that I call the Time Master. It leverages all the previously described ways to remove distractions and to get more work done and brings it all together in a cohesive mastery approach. A bit of gamification is added to spice up our working hours. My own personal experience proved that it is amazingly valid.

In this section, you'll find out:

- How the "as if" strategy can redefine your relationship with time, work, sales, and productivity. This extremely powerful approach shifts your mind-set, making it much easier to adopt more productive habits.
- How to create a transformational "as if" experiment that's fun to implement at the same time as it yields quantifiable results.

Finally, you'll have a chance to read the Time Master Manifesto, which is a call to action for everyone who wants to sell more in less time. Adopting this new mind-set will make you more efficient with less effort. For the long term.

> **GOAL:** Master the mind-set that enables you to make better decisions about time, for good.

18.

THE TIME MASTER

SOMETIMES, BY ACCIDENT, YOU STUMBLE ONTO A NEW AP-
proach that transforms everything you knew and thought about the
way you work.

After several months of being "Miss Productive," I was tired of
being so disciplined all the time. I thought it would be fun to spice
things up with a little gamification, an idea that was triggered by a
recent posting titled "Playing to Win" I'd read on the Yesware blog.
Lots of sales organizations use gamification technology these days to
spark internal motivation, create friendly competition among team
members, and boost sales. These apps track activities and closed deals.
On the leaderboards, sellers can see how they're doing vis-à-vis their
colleagues. When a rep closes a deal, bells go off, teammates are no-
tified, and congratulations are delivered. But those apps were for
teams. I was one person.

After valiantly reviewing numerous productivity apps, I didn't
find anything that got me excited. Besides, none were sales specific.
That's when I decided to create my own game. Something simple—
not one bit technical—and fun to play. For weeks I studied successful

game design, a field that was far more complex than I realized. Then I moved into creative mode, which was a delightful change of pace.

The first step was to determine the game's goal. That was easy—I wanted more sales in less time. But I also needed to create an avatar, enemies, quests to go on, levels of advancement, triggers, tracking, and rewards.

I decided to create my characters first. When I thought of my avatar (my game-playing alter ego), Buffy the Vampire Slayer popped into my head. Not liking the killer image, I tossed it out. For days, I pondered who I wanted to become when I played the time game. Slowly a new image emerged: an avatar possessing deep knowledge and magical capabilities—like a wizard. She was wearing a red cape over her long white robes and holding a staff.

Enter Jill the Time Master. A hero who could deftly outwit and stifle those enemies (like Dr. Distracto and the evil Emailia) who stole her precious time. An avatar who could also accomplish miraculous deeds efficiently and effortlessly. She wasn't faster than a speeding bullet, but she was capable of getting more done in one day than people thought was possible.

For the next few weeks I struggled to create "the game" that would change my life. It got far too complex. I didn't like being constantly at war and battling my enemies. That seemed to give them even more power over my life. Tracking was a real pain. Even rewards like a new outfit, a bottle of red wine, or an afternoon off didn't motivate me. They simply weren't sufficient to drive long-term change. Clearly I was a failure as a game designer.

One surprising thing was having an impact though. I'd written "Jill the Time Master" on a big sheet of paper and posted it on the wall in my office. Every time I'd walk in and see it, I'd smile and stand up a little straighter. It was like I was entering this absurd role and enjoying it. When I was Jill the Time Master, I got more done—and it wasn't that hard.

I thought I was losing my mind. I didn't dare tell anyone about it. After all, I'm this highly practical sort of person, not a fruitcake who spends her time in la-la land.

Flash forward one month. I'd totally given up on the game. It wasn't fun or motivational. But I was still working undercover as Jill the Time Master and getting a prodigious amount of work done. Instead of jumping right into my e-mail, I'd take a few minutes to review my calendar and really think about the day ahead. Looking at my master task list, I'd focus in on what I wanted to accomplish for the day. I'd pick out my ONE Thing and a few extra if I got time. Then I'd block the time out on my calendar so it was set in stone.

As the day went on, I'd stick to my plan. I took regular breaks. Occasionally I'd be tempted to peek at my e-mail, check out LinkedIn, or disappear into my news feed. But the Time Master gently nudged me back to my real work. Even my travel to speak at a number of annual sales meetings and conferences didn't throw me off.

As the Time Master, I valued my time more than ever. It was my biggest asset, my primary resource. Any time I lost was squandered, unavailable for future use. I also had this deep intuitive knowledge about how to plan my day, work through challenges that arose, and keep myself energized. I was more focused, more strategic, and more creative than I'd been in years.

I'll never forget when I realized that acting as if I were the Time Master might actually have some validity and that it could actually be an approach that others could use as well.

It was a beautiful September afternoon. I was out for a short walk, listening to a podcast interview with Dr. Ellen Langer, a Harvard psychology professor and the author of *Counterclockwise*. She was talking about a famous experiment she conducted with elderly men, early in her career.

Langer wanted to find out if turning the clock back psychologically could also turn it back physically. For her study, a group of elderly men were divided into two sections: the "time travelers" and the control group. Before the experiment began, she tested each one to measure their strength, posture, eyesight, cognitive skills, and more.

During the one-week study, her time travelers' charter was to relive the past. They were expected to live "as if" it were 1959, not 1979 (the actual year). On the way to the retreat center, fifties music played. When they arrived, these wobbly older men were expected to carry their own luggage to their room. After all, twenty years earlier they could do it.

While together, the time travelers watched 1950s TV programs and listened to old radio shows. "Current" issues of *Life* magazine and the *Saturday Evening Post* were strewn around. They talked about President Eisenhower, the Cold War, and sporting events from that era. All conversations had to be in the present tense—this was happening now.

The control group's charter while at the retreat center was to spend a week reminiscing about the "good old days" when they were twenty years younger. Everything surrounding them remained current as they relived what was going on in the world during the 1950s.

As the week progressed, Langer started seeing dramatic differences emerge. The time travelers walked faster and more confidently; some even threw their canes away. Their attitudes changed. Testing at the end of the experiment showed that their memories improved. So did their blood pressure, hearing, eyesight, and intelligence. In every single category, the time travelers outperformed the control group.

By acting "as if" they were twenty years younger, the time travelers became younger. They didn't have to do anything else.

I was captivated by this result because it so closely mirrored my Time Master experience. I needed to know more.

19.

THE "AS IF" PHENOMENON

WILLIAM JAMES, AN AMERICAN PHILOSOPHER, ONCE SAID, "If you want a quality, act as if you have it." But was there really scientific evidence to back it up?

According to Dr. Richard Wiseman, UK psychologist and author of *The As If Principle*, the answer is an unequivocal yes. In his book, he cites numerous studies where simply changing a behavior leads to changed emotions. For example, the act of smiling instantly makes you happier. You don't have to will yourself to be happier. You don't have to think pleasant thoughts. You just have to act "as if" you're happier by smiling, and then you are. Same thing if you need more willpower. If you simply clench your fists (which is what people do to prevent themselves from giving in to temptation), your resistance increases.

That got me thinking about several high-impact strategies I used early in my sales career. While they'd made a huge difference, I didn't tell anyone about them for years because I was embarrassed.

I used to be terrified of cold calling. I'd sit in my car for thirty minutes once I arrived at a prospect's office, unable to get out and face the unknown. One day, a song popped into my head. The lyrics suggest that when you're afraid, if you simply strike a "careless pose," no one will know how you're actually feeling. I decided to give it a try. I got out of the car and held my head erect and struck that careless pose, looking as if I was totally fine with the world. After a few minutes, I sauntered into the building feeling like a different person. What amazed me most was that people reacted to me as if I were a competent professional, so I had to act like one.

Then there were the times I "borrowed" Jim's brain. Jim was a hugely successful rep I was training under. I was intimidated by his deep knowledge and sales savvy and hoped that someday I could be like him. Whenever I got stuck, I'd take a deep breath, then ask myself, "What would Jim do?" Then I'd act like him. That easily, I was able to access ideas and problem-solving strategies that I was personally incapable of coming up with at that point in my career.

That's why I was so excited when I read about the work done by Dr. George Kelly, the Ohio State University professor who's considered the father of cognitive clinical psychology. He believed that a person's view of him- or herself could be altered in a fairly short period of time. For example, a shy person could come to see himself as outgoing. A person who continually had money problems could become financially astute. A stingy person could become generous.

In his practice, Kelly used a variety of strategies to help people define what characteristics they really wanted to possess. They'd stare at a mirror for an extended time, asking themselves, "What's the difference between the person I see and the person I'd really like to be?" They'd compare themselves to people they knew well, trying to find the traits they wanted to eliminate or add to their self-image. Then they'd actively design a new identity for themselves. Some people chose to do major makeovers, while others only made a slight tweak.

Once his patients completed the new identity design, Kelly moved them into phase 2, where they acted "as if" they already were who they wanted to be. They had to do it for two full weeks. The results? After playing this role for this relatively short period of time, people forgot they were acting. It started to feel real to them, like it really was who they were. Acting "as if" they were a different person made it easy for them to be different.

That was exactly my experience. Before I became Jill the Time Master, I'd stared at my own productivity shortcomings in the proverbial mirror. I'd spent hours studying what highly productive people did differently. I'd replicated their behaviors and definitely achieved results. But with a mental image stuck in "Jill the Time Waster" mode, it was a continual challenge to stay on task. Hard work.

By creating the Time Master, I actively designed a new identity for myself—exactly what Kelly recommended. And because it was a game I was experimenting with, I just started playing it without any angst at all.

Upon entering my office every day, I became the Time Master. I'd breathe deeply a couple of times to absorb my new wisdom. I was focused and calm. I protected myself from self-created distractions. My frenetic busyness virtually evaporated into thin air. Instead of feeling under the gun to get more work done, I was having fun finding new ways to be more productive.

After a couple of weeks, I started detaching from seeing myself as the queen of distraction. I enjoyed my noninterrupted work time and got so much more done. I slowly began to reconnect with the person inside me who used to be able to handle it all. And realized I still could, without a constant battle. As the Time Master.

That was the missing link. Knowing about productive strategies and techniques was important but not enough. Seeing yourself differently is crucial—and you don't even have to believe it's real at first. You just need to act "as if" it's true.

NEW-IDENTITY EXPERIMENT

Think of someone you know who's really productive. This person gets a lot done, but they never give the impression of being crazy busy. Take a few minutes and jot down your thoughts on how they work, think, plan, strategize, deal with challenges, and more. Then for just one day, act "as if" you're this person. When you're done, reflect on what it was like: What did you find yourself doing in your new persona? How was it different from your normal patterns of behavior?

20.

PATH OF LEAST RESISTANCE

MOVING INTO THE TIME MASTER MODE CHANGED EVERYTHING for me. I'd been trying so hard for so many months to be more productive. Yes, I'd achieved significant gains in productivity, but it felt transient. Like if I stopped paying attention, I'd slip back into my old ways.

That's why it was such a shock to have discovered that a shift in mind-set could lead to such positive behavior changes. As I reflected on the ease of the transition into my new non-crazy-busy persona, I realized that many factors were at play. I didn't just wake up one day and assume a new identity. Instead, I'd unknowingly created a foundation for success.

Here's why I believe the Time Master worked like a charm:

Depth of Knowledge. In my months of research, I'd acquired the deep knowledge necessary for making a successful transition. I'd done tons of experiments. I'd installed numerous tools to prevent me from being distracted. I knew what I needed to know. That's why I devoted the first half of this book to these strategies. In order to be a Time Master, it's essential to fully understand what highly productive people do and why it matters.

Ultimate Simplicity. Acting "as if" I were the Time Master was the ultimate in simplicity. When you're already overwhelmed and are trying to implement so many different ways of working, it's much tougher than most people realize. That's why almost everyone defaults to their status quo. But as the Time Master, all the various behaviors I was trying to change were incorporated under that umbrella term. It reduced the number of decisions I needed to make to one: What would the Time Master do?

Creating Something New. It's a lot easier to create a new habit than to get rid of bad ones. By creating the Time Master avatar, I was focusing on the future, not battling the demons of my past. My resistance to change virtually evaporated. I didn't have any Time Master neural pathways. I was creating new ones every day—and they got stronger the more I used them.

Making It Fun. Before, trying to adopt all those new skills was hard work, requiring tons of discipline. But acting "as if" I were the Time Master had a sense of ridiculousness about it. Of course, I was the only one who knew it, but it really did make me laugh as I was going through the day. When you're having a good time, you're more likely to repeat what you're doing the next day, and the next, until your new behavior actually becomes a part of you.

Short Duration. I never once said, "I'm going to behave as the Time Master for the rest of my life." It was always "just for today," because I needed to get specific work done. Without the burden of forever, I was freed to just work on today. When tomorrow came, I did it again simply because it was fun and helped me be more productive. Even today, while many of these behaviors are now incorporated into my everyday work style, I'm not always in Time Master mode. But I can turn it on in a nanosecond.

What I do know is this. Acting "as if" is a much easier way to change behavior. I didn't have to change my attitude first. I didn't even need to believe I was particularly good at being productive. I simply needed to pretend I was for a short period of time before it actually started becoming true.

I strongly encourage you to give it a try. Maybe not even on productivity first. Recently, I've wanted to lose some weight. When I went out to eat with some friends, I ordered dinner "as if" I were twenty pounds lighter. I ordered a lot less—and it was easy. That's the beauty of acting "as if."

Start by doing mini "as if" experiments. I've listed some ideas here. See how they work for you in the short term, like one meeting or event. After that, extend your experiment to a longer span of time—perhaps a full day or a week. Make sure to celebrate every little thing you do well. It helps strengthen the development of new and better habits.

When you're ready, it's time to create your own avatar, one who's hell-bent on ensuring that you're able to sell more in less time. We'll tackle that next.

MINI "AS IF" EXPERIMENTS

When you're selling, you often need to change your attitude. Research has shown that these "as if" strategies actually work. Give them a couple of minutes to take effect.

- To increase persistence: Sit up straight (no slouching) and hold your head high. This is the physicality of determined people. Don't give up too soon.
- To have more willpower: Cross your arms, make a fist, or squeeze a pencil. Tensing your muscles increases your resolve to stay the course. Sellers with grit succeed.

- To raise your confidence: Assume a power pose for two minutes before an important sales meeting or an interview. Confidence is contagious.
- To be happier: Laugh for two minutes. Not about anything in particular. Just laugh. Start with some "tee-hees" and move into "ho-hos." Happy reps accomplish more.

Take note of what you discover. See if you can find new "as if" strategies yourself.

21.

GET INTO CHARACTER

IT TOOK ME A LONG TIME TO GO PUBLIC WITH MY TIME MAS-ter persona. In fact, it wasn't until I discovered the body of research around acting "as if" that I came out of the closet, so to speak. Since that time, I've shared the story with numerous salespeople, entrepreneurs, and normal human beings. All are amazed at the power of acting "as if."

What I realize, though, is that the Time Master works because I created it specifically for me. I thought long and hard about the avatar that best represented my character. I could have chosen the Sales Master, but that wasn't the battle I was fighting. I could have chosen the Distraction Slayer, but it didn't align with my vision of myself. I wanted quiet wisdom, ease, depth; that's just more me.

The moment I settled on the Time Master, a whole new way of thinking opened up for me. That thinking inspired the Time Master Manifesto (which you'll find at the end of this chapter). It's a public declaration of my beliefs, motives, and intentions. Hopefully you find some value in it too.

As a manifesto, it's meant to be a call to action. Reading it daily inspires me to work differently than I would without it. What's most fascinating to me is that I could never have written it as myself. It took assuming a new identity to tap into the knowledge that was already inside me.

Enough about me. It's time to get you set up to try this strategy too.

"AS IF" EXPERIMENT

To make this work for you, you need to personalize this challenge. Here are the steps you can follow to activate your life-changing "game." Please note that I'm not talking about putting together the kind with enemies, levels, awards, and more. All those are unnecessary and only complicate things. This is an "as if" game that you get to play.

1. **Choose Your Quest.** All games start with a challenge. Pick one productivity challenge you want to tackle in the upcoming weeks. Perhaps you want to minimize distractions. Maybe you need to organize your days better.

2. **Create Your Avatar.** You need a persona who inspires you. This is the person you're going to become for this experiment—and hopefully find hidden inside you after a few weeks. Start by exploring these areas.
   - Today: How do you see yourself now in relation to this aspect of personal productivity? As you look in the mirror, what are your strengths and weaknesses?
   - Role Models: Think about how you want to *be*. Reflect on what you've learned in this book. Think of people you know who seem to get a lot done in a short time. What are they doing that you want to embrace in your work?

- Character: Define your avatar's character, attitudes, and be-haviors. What's important? What does he/she stand for?
- Name: Pick out a fun name that embraces your image. You could be a swashbuckling pirate, a goddess, or a *Star Wars* character.
- Reminder: Create something to help you get into the role on a daily basis. Perhaps a sign, image, or slogan—whatever helps you make the transition into your new persona.

3. **Start the Game.** Let the fun begin. Act "as if" you're your av-atar for today. Just one day—and see how it feels. You're just testing out this new image of yourself. If you run into any problems, change things. You're not a failure. This is a game. You just need to make some adjustments. Try it again the next day . . . and the next.

Every day, think about how it feels to be this avatar, what you're learning, and how you're changing. Just observe how things are different.

According to Dr. Kelly, it takes about two weeks to start see-ing yourself as possessing the traits of your new persona. Per-sonally, I say keep at it as long as it's fun and helping you get better. Make sure you celebrate every achievement too, even the small ones. Shout, "Yes!" aloud (or silently) whenever you do something right.

Acting "as if" is a whole different way of picking up new skills and behaviors. It's a mind-set that shifts how you think and act with minimal resistance. In my experience, it's the easiest and simplest way I've ever found to change.

As I said earlier, it's what led me to create this Time Master Manifesto, which I now live by.

TIME MASTER MANIFESTO

I create my life, rather than let life just happen to me.

I value my time. It's all I have. When it's gone, I'll never get it back.

I wake up each day refreshed, ready to start my work joyfully.

I begin my day with what matters most. I'm clear on my priorities.

I think about what I'm doing and why. Frenetic busyness is craziness.

I work in blocks of time. This gets me in the flow.

I embrace tools that help me get more done or protect me from myself.

I schedule my entire day in my calendar and adjust as needed.

I create fun challenges to get me started and achieve my goals.

I constantly experiment, finding better ways to do every aspect of my job.

I treat myself to fun, energy-renewing breaks throughout the day.

I prevent distractions by sitting quietly till they pass.

I don't do everything. I delegate or say no.

I reflect at the end of each day.

I accept my responsibility for creating the life I want. It's up to me.

Download the Time Master Manifesto PDF at
www.jillkonrath.com/time-master.

PART 5
ADD THE
SECRET SAUCE

We are not robots. We're human beings who bring our whole being to work. To perform at our optimal level, the factors in this section are just as essential as minimizing distractions and designing an efficient workday. Perhaps they're even more important because they're what gives us life.

Unfortunately, these secret-sauce ideas are frequently ignored in our crazy-busy, results-driven sales organizations. The push is always to work harder, make more calls, sell more stuff. People brag about how many hours they put in and how little sleep they got. When stressed out, they're told to "man up" and to deal with it. If only it were that simple. Again, we're human beings.

In this section, you'll discover numerous secret-sauce strategies to:

- Energize you and make you feel better. When life is good, optimism rises. When your future feels positive, sales go up. It's a nice cycle, and true.

- Enhance your thinking. You not only need a clear mind to do this job well, you also need fresh perspectives and new options to deal with the inevitable challenges we face on a regular basis.

These strategies significantly impact your productivity and your performance. Although they're not typically talked about in a sales culture, they should be. They truly are the secret sauce that underlies everything we do. Neglect them at your own peril.

GOAL: Increase the quality of your work—
and how you feel about it.

22.

WORK WORTH DOING

AS HUMAN BEINGS—AND SALESPEOPLE—WE HAVE AN IN-
trinsic need to feel that what we do makes a difference. The truth is
nobody can stay motivated for an extended period of time if they're
just pounding the phones, blasting prospects with spammy e-mail
messages, or delivering canned pitches. We start feeling like robotic
selling machines. External attempts to make us more productive—
like spiffs, leaderboards, games, blitzes, and bonuses—at best yield
short-term spikes in performance.

We've already talked about the importance of knowing your
"why" when it comes to your goal of selling more in less time. Your
ability to achieve that can be accelerated by knowing what you sell
has a positive impact on others. It's a force multiplier.

Adam Grant, Wharton School professor and author of *Give and
Take*, researched call center workers whose job was to phone school
alumni in the evenings and request donations for future scholarship
recipients. In his experiment, he broke the callers into two groups.
For the control group, nothing changed. But the other group had a

chance to meet a person who'd actually benefitted from these fund-raising efforts.

A month later, the impact on those call center employees who'd actually met the scholarship recipient was striking. They worked harder, making twice as many calls per hour. Plus, they quintupled the amount they raised. Prior to the meeting it was $400 a week; afterward it was $2,000 a week.

Here's the deal. Knowing the difference we make has a huge impact on our productivity and success.

Recently I spoke at Rimini Street's sales kickoff meeting. Their salespeople (and entire company) are on a mission to free prospects from the bondage of the giant technology companies who charge outrageous software maintenance fees. Their clients typically save 1.5 times what they're spending annually. But it's more than that. They give significantly better service. On a scale of 1 to 5, customers rate Rimini Street as a 4.8. Plus, their clients can use their savings to fund innovative projects that would give them a competitive edge. Is it any wonder these reps are motivated to work hard and the company is on a rapid growth trajectory?

Medtronic is a global leader in medical technology and services. When I interviewed the VP of sales for one of their business units, tears actually came to his eyes as he spoke about how patients' lives changed after being implanted with their medical device. He shared story after story. He told me his whole team felt that way—and that they were growing by leaps and bounds, connected as they were to their company's impact on real people.

At Media Junction, a website design firm, CEO Trish Lessard and her team are totally committed to having a quantifiable impact on their clients' businesses. I know because they recently updated my website. Not only am I delighted with how it looks, but it also success-fully repositioned me in the market and is attracting more leads. Today, the home page of Media Junction's website proclaims, "We build custom websites & our clients think we're pretty damn good at it." They're right—and they're also growing like gangbusters.

Far too many companies today don't educate their salespeople about the value they deliver. They think that what sells is their exciting technology, extraordinary service, or innovative approach. They're wrong... and they don't even know it. The only way you can get a prospect to change is by having a strong value proposition that clearly articulates the business outcomes a company gets when they use your offering.

If you don't know the difference your company makes, take some time to learn about it. The payback will be huge. The best thing to do is to interview your clients, especially the ones who have chosen to do business with you in the past six to twelve months. Find out how you've helped them. Ask them about the results they've achieved. Explore how what you do has increased revenue, reduced costs, improved efficiency, or minimized risk. Then start using this info in your e-mails, phone messages, conversations, presentations, and proposals.

Most of all, use the findings as a personal motivator. You are helping people. You are making a difference. You are doing work that matters.

I even have to keep reminding myself about that. Writing books is hard, I'm not a natural speaker, and clearly I struggle with productivity. But I keep at it because I know my efforts contribute to a better world. As Tom Rath, author of *Are You Fully Charged?*, says, "Work is a purpose, not a place."

VALUE IMMERSION EXERCISE

Identify one client to interview, preferably one who started using your product or service not too long ago and is already seeing results. Tell your contact that you really want to understand how your offering is impacting their business. Before talking, prepare questions around the key impact areas and use them to guide your conversation. Be interested and curious. Be willing to go "off script" too and explore areas of value that you might not have even known about.

23.

A REAL WAKE-UP CALL

I WAS IN BOSTON TO SPEAK AT HUBSPOT'S BIG INBOUND CON-
ference. During the opening keynote, publisher Arianna Huffington
spoke about leadership, success, and . . . sleep. She shared stories
about how lack of pillow time led to poor decisions, reduced productivity, and health issues. She talked about sleep's virtues—creativity,
energy, fresh thinking. We all laughed when she dropped her most
memorable line: "Sleep is a performance-enhancement tool. It's time
to sleep our way to the top."

So many sellers today are working their butts off, trying to meet
their numbers. Add in everything else that's important to them and
something has to give. Often it's sleep.

For most of my adult life, I've said, "I can get by on six and a half
hours of sleep." By that, I meant that I believed I could bring my best
me to work and do a great job. Consequently, I'd stay up late and get
up early, making sure I got my minimum and even a little more. (I'm
not a great sleeper.)

Now that I was trying to get more done in less time, I was questioning if those hours were enough. Huffington's talk was replaying in my head, but I wanted to check out the research myself.

The first thing I discovered was that I wasn't alone in my sleep habits. In a Gallup study, Americans reported that they averaged 6.8 hours nightly—a full hour less than seventy years ago. In another study done by Diane Lauderdale at the University of Chicago, the 669 middle-aged adults she was researching reported they got 7.5 hours per night. But after she tested them over a period of time using wrist monitors, it turned out they were really only getting 6.1 hours.

Does the extra hour or two matter? According to scientists, the answer is a resounding yes. Our brain is busy working most of the night. In fact, 80 percent of the time we're sleeping, our brain is more active than during the day. It's filing away new information. It's replaying over and over what we've been learning to ensure it sticks. It's looking for fresh ways to solve our toughest business and personal challenges.

Here's what is really disturbing. If we don't get "enough" sleep, it's harder for us to concentrate on our work. We prefer to do more mindless tasks and we get easily distracted. When we're learning something new, it actually takes much longer too. Lack of sleep even slows down our digestion, which means our brain doesn't get the glucose it needs to operate at an optimal level.

That was not what I wanted to hear. I was quite comfortable with my bedtime and sleep routines. I didn't want to change any more nasty habits of mine. But I decided to do a little experiment and figure out how the amount of sleep I got each night impacted my productivity.

Initially, I guesstimated my hours of sleep to my best ability. About a week into the experiment, I got a Fitbit so I was better able to track my sleep time. While not perfect, it gave me a pretty good daily report on how much time I slept, was awake, and was restless.

For the next thirty days I tracked how my sleep impacted my productivity. I paid special attention to how I felt each morning, the kind of work I tackled, and how effective I was. Here's a sampling of various days from my log.

6.5 hours: Woke up early. Tried to get back to sleep but finally got up. Even after three cups of coffee, brain not firing on all cylinders. Taking forever to get things done.

7 hours: Felt groggy when I woke up. Had a couple cups of coffee, checked e-mail, played Words with Friends before I forced myself to go for a walk. I was in a mental fog for 1.5 miles. Then finally fresh ideas started emerging.

5 hours: Utterly worthless today—a total zombie.

7.75 hours: Felt groggy initially, but didn't stay long. Got to work really fast today. Very productive day. Got lots done.

6 hours: Couldn't sleep because had early flight. Intended to work on plane, but got just a fraction of it done. Too hard to focus. Now I'm behind.

7.5 hours: Power-packed morning; lots of meetings scheduled so had to kick into gear. Lost some steam as the day went on.

8 hours: Super productive within thirty minutes. Amazing.

After I did this for a month, it became glaringly obvious to me that my sleep (or rather the lack of it) was really impacting my productivity. If I got more than 7.75 hours, I had a great day. I was unstoppable. If I got less than seven hours, the quality and quantity of my work really suffered.

Clearly I needed to make some changes. This time I actually wanted to because the difference I felt was so profound. But change is never easy. Based on the recommendations of numerous sleep researchers, here's what I started doing differently:

- Set a specific bedtime—just like when you were a kid—and stick to it. If you get up at 6:30 a.m., plan on going to bed at 10 p.m. If you want 8 hours of sleep, the experts say you need to plan to have 8.5 hours. The extra half hour is your grace time to wind down and fall asleep. I'm in bed by 11 p.m.
- Avoid blue light–emitting devices (phone, computer, tablet) for two hours before bedtime. If you don't, falling asleep is harder, REM sleep is shorter, and in the morning you'll be less alert. To reduce this bad light at night, I use f.lux (Night Filter for Android) on my laptop. Also, smaller devices emit less light, and you can always turn the brightness down.
- Don't work right up until bedtime. Shut down at least an hour before your bedtime to allow your mind to relax. You don't want to be tossing and turning in the middle of the night because you're trying to figure out a knotty sales challenge.
- Keep a pen and pad by your bed. If ideas and thoughts pop up as you're settling into sleep, write them down. That way you'll remember them in the morning, but they won't keep you awake. Recently I got a pen with a built-in LED light so I can write in the dark. I love it!

My sleep habits are improving because I'm focusing on them. When I slip up or have a bad night, I immediately feel the negative impact on my productivity, thinking, and even mood. I'm trying to sleep my way to the top.

SLEEP-TRACKING EXPERIMENT

Track your sleep for thirty days. Notice how your sleep patterns impact your productivity, clarity of mind, creativity, problem-solving ability, and attitude. Ask, "How much sleep do I need to perform at my best? Where do I see a drop-off?"

24.

GET YOUR OOMPH BACK

WHEN YOU FEEL SWAMPED, THE NATURAL INCLINATION IS TO dig in and work harder. This works for a short while, but over time it's unsustainable. You become worn down, lose perspective, quit growing, and don't have the energy to do much else. So in the evenings, when all else is done, you channel surf on the TV or zone out on your device—which does nothing to revitalize you.

That was my life for a while. I didn't like it but didn't know how else to cope with my overwhelming workload. Then one day, a curious thing started to happen. I started to reflect on all those years when I'd been able to handle it all more successfully. When my kids were young, I coached two Destination Imagination (DI) teams at schools, a program that focused on creative problem-solving skills. From the start of the school year to the regional competition in February, each team met weekly for three hours. Every meeting required hours of preparation. Additionally, I ran the entire high school program of nine teams.

When my kids outgrew DI, I started judging regional competitions, joined the state advisory board, and launched fresh fund-raising initiatives. With friends, I started a nonprofit for women, created the website, launched a twice-monthly newsletter, and worked on programming. When the economy crashed in 2008, I wrote a book and launched an eighteen-month initiative to help people get back to work faster. For fun, I played in a racquetball league several times a week.

How could I do all that in my spare time and not feel overwhelmed? As I thought about it, I realized that all these "time sucking" activities actually:

- Energized me. So much so that I went way beyond what was expected of me as a volunteer.
- Upped my productivity. Because of all my commitments, I needed to work smarter. I couldn't lollygag and putz around with nonessential activities.
- Expanded me. I invested tons of free time learning new things, many of which spilled over into my work, making me much better at what I do.

Rather than draining me, this "extra" work actually invigorated me. I was happy doing it. Now I'd become a drudge. I didn't have time to volunteer. Nor did I have time for fun anymore.

The only way to handle a complex lifestyle is to do things that give you your oomph back. Volunteer work makes us feel like we're making a difference. In fact, recent Wharton studies show that volunteering our time actually increases our sense of unhurried leisure. Psychological scientist Cassie Mogilner's research shows that giving away time also boosts one's sense of personal competence and efficiency too.

We need to have something to look forward to. It restores us. So does tackling new challenges. We lift our spirits when we work on a hobby, get outside, play games, or just plain do something we love.

Several years ago, my daughter Katie started playing underwater hockey (yes, there is such a thing). Today she practices twice a week, competes in tournaments across North America, and even played in the world championship in South Africa. She loves being so involved; it inspires her to get her work done faster.

Just ask Shawn Achor, Harvard psychologist and author of *The Happiness Advantage*. His research shows that a person who's feeling positive performs better at virtually every single business outcome. In his TEDx Talk, he says, "Your intelligence rises, your creativity rises, your energy levels rise. In fact . . . your brain at positive is thirty-one percent more productive than your brain at negative, neutral, or stressed. You're thirty-seven percent better at sales."

Instead of working hard, hoping that we'll find happiness, we need to reverse the formula. We need to build things into our schedule that will make us feel good inside first.

Life can't be all work. Our sales numbers aren't the only things that matter. We need to play too. For us goal-oriented, driven sales types, this can be a real challenge. We want to beat our competitors. We want to be at the top of the leaderboard, no matter what we're doing.

According to Dr. Stuart Brown, founder of the National Institute for Play, the key is to focus on the experience rather than on accomplishing a goal. You can play a joke, play an instrument, play a game, play with your kids/pets, or even go to a play. At work, you can liven up a dull meeting, goof off with a coworker, or role-play a funny sales scenario. You might also make a game out of things you don't like to do but need to get done.

Being playful triggers creativity, helps you see problems in new ways, builds stronger relationships, and gives you more energy.

This is contrarian advice for those of us who are overwhelmed, but it's much needed if we want to sell more in less time. I've taken it to heart. I now schedule time on my calendar for things that energize me. I'm getting involved again in initiatives that inspire me, even when I don't have the time. And I've already blocked time on my calendar for the trip I want to take next summer. These are not "guilty pleasures." They help me work at my best level.

GIVE-IT-AWAY EXPERIMENT

Volunteer in one non-work-related activity this week—even if it's only for an hour. Help a neighbor, family member, or colleague. Support a good cause. Every time you do this, you get more in return.

25.

FIND SOME HELP

AT CEB'S ANNUAL CONFERENCE IN 2015, THE HOT TOPIC WAS dealing with today's overwhelmed buyer. The key piece of advice was the need for sellers to make the decision process as simple as possible, a topic I'd written about extensively in *SNAP Selling*.

After the event, I spoke with Nick Toman and Brent Adamson, coauthors of *The Challenger Customer*, about the focus of CEB's next major research project. They both told me their new area of study was "the overwhelmed salesperson." In a follow-up conversation a few months later, we talked about the increasing complexity of a sales job, the need for sellers to manage a vast array of people within their own organization as well as outside, and the ongoing struggle to keep up with changes in technology, the marketplace, and more.

According to Toman, CEB's research showed that top-performing companies zealously focused on simplicity for their salespeople too. Their explicit goal was to maximize time on highly productive sales activities (research, preparation, strategizing, and meetings). To do this, they eliminated busywork like data entry or looking up e-mail addresses by adding support services, technology, or tools to off-load those tasks. The goal was to eliminate as many activities as they could that took up reps' time or mental energy.

Unfortunately, most of us don't work for companies like that. We get bogged down with issues such as resolving customer problems, handling billing issues, getting the legal department's approval, and finding the right resources. Not only is that a colossal waste of our precious time, but it also increases our stress levels. When we're feeling that way, our ability to think creatively and strategically tanks too, which means we're not as good as we should be.

We need help—and we need to ask for it. Most of us are reticent to do so, thinking, *It's our job*. Think again. It's really your job to make sales.

If you're new, you might even wait longer before asking for help. You don't want to look like you're incapable of doing your job. But remember, you're new. You're not expected to know how everything works in the company. You don't know who can solve problems. If you don't get help, you'll waste a ton of time with the wrong people, getting the wrong directions and making things even worse.

INTERNAL ROADBLOCKS

Sometimes the best place to start is to talk to your peers. Find out how they manage to shepherd contracts through the legal department, deal with tough customer issues, or get the technical resources needed to customize a solution. Check to find out if you're working with the right people in the company too.

If you don't get any fresh ideas, it's time to get your boss on board, clearing the path for you, resolving any friction, and freeing up your time for high-value sales activities. But you can't go barging in, demanding help. That'll backfire on you. Nor do you want to do it in a way that makes you look inadequate or like a martyr.

How you frame the conversation is crucial. This is about making your numbers—something your boss agrees is important. When you describe what's happening, make sure you stick with the facts, keep your emotions out of it, and don't blame anybody. Finally, know what you want your boss to do. Your request should specify the action that needs to be taken and the time frame. Here's how a conversation might go:

> **You:** Hey, boss! I need your help. I'm doing my best to close Goliath Systems by the end of the quarter but am having some challenges.
>
> **Boss:** I'm glad to hear things are moving along at Goliath. What's up though?
>
> **You:** I'm having a problem with . . .
>
>> Here's what I've already done . . .
>> If this isn't addressed, I'm concerned that . . .
>> I need your help with . . . (specific action plus time frame)

Your boss needs this information to help you out and hopefully remove the bottleneck. Personally, I've seen this strategy work wonders, so much so that I often wondered why I didn't use it earlier. Hubris, I suspect. I didn't want to look like I was incompetent.

STRATEGICALLY STUMPED

Speaking of not looking stupid, no one ever said you had to go it alone. Yet all too often, sellers are reticent to get input from others when they're facing an unfamiliar or difficult sales challenge. There's no way we can know it all. If we haven't run into a particular sales scenario before, we may be clueless as to our options.

We can get help from a variety of sources, if we just ask. Here's a huge caveat though: if you ask for help, you can't be defensive. Saying, "I've done that" over and over just shuts people down. Instead you have to stay curious, trying to find what you might have missed.

- Start with your peers. With their deep understanding of what you're selling and to whom, they can often offer suggestions that you haven't thought of. Also, since they're not so vested in the outcome, they can be far more objective than you can.
- Talk with colleagues in other departments. Think about engaging a sales engineer, marketing, customer service, HR, or the CFO to get new insights on your work. Their fresh perspectives can open your eyes to new possibilities. If you're selling to IT, perhaps someone from your own IT organization can shed some light on why a deal might be stuck and what you can do to get it moving again.
- External resources can be invaluable too. My good friend Google has given me countless ideas, and quickly too. Over the years, I've also been involved in mastermind groups. Comprised of people from related specialties, we'd get together once a month either in person, on the phone, or via an online meeting.

  Each person would get a specified amount of time to (1) share their challenge, (2) answer questions posed by other group members who needed more clarity, and (3) get feedback and ideas from the group. During this last segment, we were only allowed to take notes and at the end, thank everyone.

It's easy to get stumped when the business environment changes too. Even top sellers get thrown for a loop when new competitors emerge, recessions hit, or interest rates skyrocket. During times like these, it's a good idea to get your whole team together on a regular basis to brainstorm new approaches and share what's working. Don't try to go it alone.

UNPRODUCTIVE WORK

Today there are hundreds of productivity-enhancing sales tools available like LinkedIn, InsideView, HubSpot Sales, join.me, Yesware, and DocuSign that can save tons of time, provide you with crucial insights, and increase your effectiveness. But these tools cost money, and leadership may be wary of adopting them for a variety of reasons. They're not sure if the investment is worth it. They're intimidated by the technology. Or they're afraid of sales rebellions.

Many of these tools are available for a small monthly fee, some less than ten dollars a month. If your company won't pay for them, spend your own money. It's worth it. You'll get further ahead by investing in these tools than doing it the old way.

Consider also proposing an experiment. Talk to your boss about how you're currently doing things and the time/effort required. Show that you've analyzed the problem. Then, bring up the new sales tool, explaining its capabilities and how you think it could help. Offer to test it for the next few months to see if it makes a difference, promising to report back on what you've learned. This is especially important if the tool is tied into the CRM system.

Everyone likes experiments and is curious about their results. Plus, it will motivate you to get the most value you can from the tool—which ultimately leads to better sales results in less time.

ASK-FOR-HELP EXPERIMENT

Quick. Write down one thing you could really use some help with right now. Take a few minutes to think about who can help you with it. Then ask for help graciously—via text, e-mail, IM, or phone. When you get a response, be appreciative.

26.

DO ABSOLUTELY NOTHING

WHEN I ARRIVED AT THE MARRIOTT MARQUIS IN SAN FRAN-cisco on a Saturday afternoon in 2015, the place was packed. I'd stumbled into the Wisdom 2.0 conference, a mega-event focused on how people can live with technology without it engulfing us. LinkedIn's CEO, Jeff Weiner, was keynoting but his talk wasn't about the value of LinkedIn. Instead, his focus was on why mindfulness is important for leaders. As I have since discovered, lots of senior executives across a variety of industries are embracing mindfulness practices like meditation and yoga.

To clarify, mindfulness is about quieting the constant chatter in your head. (Harvard research shows that we're lost in thought almost 47 percent of the time.) Mindfulness seeks to stop the incessant replay about what's already happened or what could happen in the future by replacing it with a focus on now. Right now.

Recent studies have shown that these practices truly do make a difference in your life. David Levy, professor at the University of Washington, found that people who practiced meditation stayed on task longer and were less distracted. That sure boosts productivity.

In Wisconsin, neuroscientist Richard Davidson from the Center for Healthy Minds found that mindfulness helped people to be more flexible in their thinking, to come up with more creative ideas, to better control their emotions, to be more empathetic, and to feel better. Definitely assets when you're selling.

Yet in sales, you never hear about the value of mindfulness. In our hard-charging, we-need-results-now sales cultures, it feels like the antithesis of what we should be doing. We feel a compelling need to take immediate action instead of sitting quietly and doing nothing. We get antsy when we try new things, especially if they don't deliver immediate results.

In the past few years, I've experimented with being mindful and quieting my mind on a daily basis but it never quite stuck. But my interest was rekindled when I read this comment on my blog written by Carolyn Gsell:

> My entire year has been spent juggling my software sales job with cancer treatments. This is my 5th year with my current employer and I've had the best sales year ever. Yet I worked significantly fewer hours. How did I do it? I learned to meditate regularly—an hour every morning before even touching the phone and computer.

I immediately reached out to Carolyn via e-mail to learn more. When we talked, she described her precancer self as the "Energizer Bunny." But multiple surgeries and chemo sapped her energy and clouded her mind. She finally decided that things had to change. Specifically, she decided that for six weeks, she was only going to work in the morning. Afternoons were set aside for relaxing activities like reading, writing, and reflecting. At the end of her six weeks, she was a very different person. Quiet. Calm. Focused on key priorities.

Going back to work full time, Carolyn committed to meditating each morning as well as monitoring her energy. If she's tired, she takes a nap. Now, she says, "I've learned how to get way more done with doing a lot less. My creativity has skyrocketed. I'm actually enjoying my work and had the most financially rewarding year of my life." By simply slowing down and doing nothing, she's at the peak of her career.

Wanting to learn more, I reached out to the only sales guru I know who talks about and practices mindful selling: Jonathan London, CEO of Improved Performance Group. He told me, "When you quiet your mind, your presence actually changes. Rather than focusing on your agenda (or your fears), you're calmer, more compassionate and empathetic with your prospects. They feel safer, understood and unrushed—and they trust you more."

According to London, even just a few minutes of mindfulness prior to a sales meeting can transform everything. He suggests pausing to take a few deep breaths while you feel your butt in the chair and your feet on the floor. You can also pay attention to the noise in the office, to what is happening now versus only your thoughts. Let go of tension. When you meet with your prospect, you'll be more relaxed and more sincerely focused on their needs—all of which yields better sales results.

Could just a few minutes really make a difference? Previously, when I'd tried to practice mindfulness, I thought I needed to start each day with at least twenty to thirty minutes of meditation. When you've never done it before, that's an eternity. My mind was racing ahead, planning the day, and remembering things I needed to do. Random thoughts on totally irrelevant topics bubbled up from nowhere. I kept checking the clock to see how much time I had left. The glorious promises of doing nothing never materialized. Instead, I was frustrated and irritable, wondering why I even bothered to waste the time. On busy days (most of them), I just couldn't seem to get around to it. Imagine that!

I decided to try another experiment. This time, I'd follow B. J. Fogg's advice to focus on "tiny habits." I signed up for his free five-day e-mail course and selected the new habits I wanted to add to my life. According to Fogg, the best way to learn a new habit is to tie it into something you do every day. That's your anchor for triggering the new behavior. Using his very specific formula for success, I picked this mindfulness habit.

> After I sit down at my desk, I'll sit quietly for a short while be-
> fore I open my computer.

The anchor (sitting at my desk) triggers the new habit (mindfulness). I didn't put any time frame on it, because I wanted to keep this exercise as simple as possible. Otherwise I'd be checking the clock or wondering when my silent time was over.

The first time I practiced my new habit, I truly enjoyed it—which shocked the living daylights out of me. By the time I went online, I was much calmer and more focused on what I needed to get done. So far, I've kept up this mini mindfulness habit and I'm even expanding it. Additionally, during the day, I'll sometimes pause to sit quietly and check in with myself.

In a post on his LinkedIn blog, CEO Jeff Weiner wrote that the "single most important productivity tool" he uses is making time in his schedule each day to clear his mind and do nothing. Hard as that might be for us action-oriented sellers, I think he's on to something.

DO-NOTHING EXPERIMENT

Identify one habit that you do every single workday that you can use as the anchoring trigger for the new "do nothing" habit you want to try out. Examples of your trigger could be finding your seat on the train, pouring a cup of coffee, getting the kids off to school, or sitting down at your desk. Write it down using B. J. Fogg's formula:

After I [insert anchor], I will [insert new behavior].

Each day, for one week, as soon as you complete the trigger, do nothing. Breathe deeply and slowly. Stare out your window or at a picture you like. Appreciate the day and just do nothing—for a short time. When you're done, notice how you feel and think. If it makes a difference, next week do it a little longer or do it more times each day.

27.

WALKING IS WORK

HAVE YOU EVER FOUND YOURSELF STARING AT YOUR COM- puter, trying to come up with a way to get into that big account, but you feel totally brain-dead? Or maybe your best prospect has disappeared into a black hole and you've tried every option you know to reconnect. Or perhaps a dreaded competitor is making inroads with your top client and you need to figure out how to handle the situation but nothing comes to mind.

When we get stuck, most of us default to checking our e-mail or doing something equally distracting. After a few minutes, we're back facing the same problem again in no better position than before. We sit at our desk, willing ourselves to find the answer, but none emerges.

When you hit an impasse like this, it's time to reignite your cubicle brain. You need to stand up, move away from that desk, and get your body in motion. Take a good walk—I'm talking at least twenty to thirty minutes, because you're looking for some fresh ideas and they don't just pop out in a five-minute jaunt.

Several years ago, I stumbled onto the power of a good walk during the workday. Although I get out and walk a lot, I never did it during business hours. But for some reason, I headed out midday to just enjoy the nice weather. About fifteen minutes into my walk, it was like something unlocked my brain. Suddenly a great idea for a project popped into my mind. Then I got to thinking about which of my clients might find the most value in it. By the time I arrived home, I knew who I was going to call, how I was going to pitch the concept, and the pricing. That two-mile walk yielded a very profitable piece of business, virtually in the course of a half hour.

I started to make walks during business hours a daily habit. It pulls me away from the nitty-gritty of my work and gets me thinking at a higher, more creative level. Sometimes I'll even pose a question to myself before I head out the door and then let it go.

You are not being a slacker if you do this; you're being smart. According to John Medina, author of *Brain Rules*, our brains are built for walking twelve miles a day—which is what early man did. We function better when we're moving. Yet according to the *British Journal of Sports Medicine*, the average office worker sits for ten hours a day—commuting, doing e-mail, making calls, eating lunch, and writing proposals. That doesn't even include the evenings. To maintain our health—and our minds—we should be moving for at least two hours during our time at work, but preferably four.

Taking a nice walk pumps up your brain's oxygen levels. That, in turn, brings more glucose to the brain and reduces the toxic waste generated by processing it. So you're getting more fuel and getting rid of the junk.

Better yet, walking improves your ability to come up with new ideas. Recently, two Stanford researchers, Marily Oppezzo and Daniel Schwartz, found that a person's creativity increased by an average of 60 percent when walking instead of sitting. It didn't matter if the person was walking indoors on a treadmill or outside. Even better, creative juices continued to flow even when subjects got back to their desks.

When you're sitting in front of your computer, your brain is actually doing a very focused type of thinking. It's looking for the right answer. When you're walking, you're not only getting more fuel to your brain, but are actually moving it into a different mode. It relaxes, steps back, and takes a thirty-thousand-foot approach.

During that time, without you even knowing it, your brain is busy searching for bits of knowledge and ideas it has stored in all its various and sundry parts. It remembers a strategy you used long ago. It recalls an article that had some interesting and relevant insights. It searches for possible answers, options, and ideas. That's why we need to walk when we're stuck. We think better.

Business innovator and author Nilofer Merchant recently gave a hugely popular TED Talk in which she made the pronouncement that "sitting has become the smoking of our generation." Several years ago she switched one meeting from a coffee shop to a walking meeting. She enjoyed it so much that she now does it on a regular basis, averaging twenty to thirty miles per week. She says that it's great for out-of-the-box thinking and that it brings an entirely new set of ideas into your life.

Next time you have some things to discuss with colleagues, see if they'd like to go for a walking meeting. As Merchant says, "Fresh air drives fresh thinking." You'll also find that people are more candid, you'll have a more honest exchange of ideas, and you'll build stronger relationships.

Cubicle brains can't come up with game-changing strategies or new ways to solve challenging problems. You need to get walking during the business day. You'll be much more productive than you ever could have been if you'd sat at your desk.

PS: I'm from Minnesota, where it's bitterly cold for months on end. If I can do it, so can you.

MAKE-A-MOVE EXPERIMENT

Next time you're stumped or looking for fresh ideas, go for a thirty-minute walk. If you need a colleague's input, go for a walk together. Remove yourself from the work environment to find the answers you're looking for.

28.

SET UP FOR SUCCESS

OUR WORK SPACE HAS A HUGE IMPACT ON OUR PRODUCTIV-
ity, in many different ways. Some of us work out of a home office where
we have total control over our environment. Others are working in
crowded offices where our colleagues are right on top of one another.
You may be much more limited in what you can change. Still, there
are changes that everyone can make to create an optimal work environment.

MINIMIZE HUMAN INTERRUPTIONS

Whether you're in a high-density office or working at home, you're
virtually guaranteed to be interrupted multiple times during the day.
Sometimes it's a welcome break; other times it's a major distraction.
Even someone asking for a "quick minute" can cause you to lose twenty
to thirty minutes of productivity.

Over the years, when I truly want peace and quiet so I can concentrate, I've learned to warn people around me who could likely interrupt. I put a Post-it note on my office door that says, "BUSY! Do Not

Interrupt." Sometimes I stick up an extra note that lets people know when I'll be free.

If you're in a crowded office, you need other strategies. In numerous companies I've visited, salespeople use noise-cancelling headphones to signal that they want to be left alone. Concurrently, they might be listening to Focus@Will (a favorite app of mine) to drown out the ambient noise and enhance productivity.

At Fifth Column Games, CEO Andrew Marsh and his team place "cones of silence" on their desks to indicate they're hard at work. I've also seen some fun photos online of people who've taped "Do Not Disturb" signs to their own backs to stop others from interrupting them.

Another key strategy used by savvy sellers is to move to a different location where they can't be disturbed. They frequently book office conference rooms or escape to the local coffee shop to think, strategize, and plan.

Finally, we have to deal with bosses who want us to stop everything to get them a report or update right now. Yes, I know they're under pressure too, and sometimes what they request is truly urgent. However, most of the time it's not. Talk to your boss ahead of time about how hard you're working to improve your sales productivity and the high cost of interruptions. Then, when a request comes in to do something now, it's easy to say, "Can I get to it in thirty minutes? I'm putting together a proposal right now and don't want to lose my train of thought."

REORGANIZE YOUR WORK SPACE

For me, walking into my office every day was like entering a disaster zone. My desk had piles of project folders, receipts, and Post-it notes (which I use to jot down ideas) scattered everywhere. My floor was stacked with books that I couldn't manage to fit onto my overflowing shelves. I could feel myself being distracted by the visible clutter that lay everywhere.

While it had never really bugged me before, now I was irritated. I was turning into a minimalist. Less felt better. One afternoon, I finally took action. Setting my timer for twenty-five minutes, I took absolutely everything off my desk and gave it a good wipe down.

Then, as I began putting things back on it, I started asking questions like, Do I really need this? Can I digitize it or toss it? Where does it belong? I even threw out pens that I hated and meaningless knickknacks. At the end, I'd created a much better work space. I had a small "to be continued" box for everything I needed to tackle later. I had a pile of books to take to Goodwill. The process wasn't completed, but it was a good start and I immediately felt the difference.

I didn't make my work space barren though. Research by the University of Exeter showed office workers' productivity was boosted by up to 35 percent if they were able to personalize their work space. In mine, I have meaningful quotes and a few art objects posted on the wall. Photos of my family and trips we've taken are on my credenza. And there's a big cat tree in the corner for Cali, who spends the afternoons with me.

RETHINK YOUR DIGITAL WORK SPACE

Recently, I posted a question in my LinkedIn group asking, "How many monitors/screens/tabs do you have open on your computer right now? What's on them?"

James M. confessed that on his desktop he had ten file managers (stacked) open, one web browser with twenty tabs open (twelve pinned), one web-based e-mail account, Outlook e-mail with three accounts, PowerPoint, Evernote, Notepad, Media Player, and a graphics program. Sharon A. stated that she had thirteen screens open on two monitors. Open apps included Salesforce, LinkedIn, Gmail, Outlook, websites for researching, PowerPoint, Excel, Word, her company's site, and several related pieces of company information.

Earlier we talked about the importance of focus, working in only one app or on one task at a time. While that's ideal, sometimes it's impossible. In our role as sellers, we often need to use multiple apps concurrently while we research clients online, take notes, toggle between screens, and communicate with others. It can get confusing.

Personally, I "felt" better and more productive when I added a big monitor to my setup, but I had no idea that there was research to back it up. Yet according to a Microsoft study, users are at least 9 percent more productive with a bigger screen—or multiple screens. The additional real estate makes it easier for people to go back and forth between tasks. It prevents them from accidentally closing files and minimizes time spent resizing windows and finding the one to bring to the forefront.

Jake Reni, a sales leader at Consensus, takes his screens seriously. He knows that they impact his productivity, for better or worse. Recently, he moved to a three-screen configuration to optimize his time. Here's how he's organized things:

- The left screen is dedicated to what he's actually working on: e-mail, calendars, and his demo environment.
- In the middle is his "accountability screen," which includes Salesforce, Trello (project management), Slack (team messaging), and Evernote (for storing/viewing saved information).
- On his right is the "distraction screen," which he uses for his social selling activities. It includes LinkedIn Sales Navigator, Hootsuite (social listening and tweeting), and Spotify (music).

According to Jake, this distraction screen can be a total black hole and he could spend hours there. That's why he moved it off his main work area so he doesn't look at it till he's ready. He also uses numerous other productivity apps to simplify his work.

There's no optimum number of monitors or apps you should be using to create the best work environment. What's most important is that you think about the best way to get your work done with a minimal number of distractions.

We need to consider if we're set up for success—and address any obstacles preventing us from doing our best work. Do you need to make changes in your work space? Are you ready to deal with the inevitable interruptions?

PET PEEVE EXPERIMENT

We all have at least one distraction that drives us crazy. Whether it's a messy desk, a noisy office, or a specific coworker, it interferes with our ability to sell more in less time. Rather than letting it happen again, for one day decide to do something about it. You know it's coming, so put together a plan. Or put some time on your calendar to take care of it. You have more control than you think.

PART 6
ACCELERATE SALES

To sell more in less time, it's imperative to look beyond minimizing distractions and optimizing time to new sales strategies that can help you capture prospects' attention, keep deals moving, and land bigger contracts.

To succeed, it's essential to upgrade your thinking, deepen your knowledge, and enhance your skills. By doing so, you'll have a significantly higher close rate than your peers and competitors.

In this section, you'll discover how to:

- Target accounts with immediate needs who are ready to take action . . . in a much shorter time frame than normal. You'll also get insights into what it takes to pursue bigger, more profitable deals, which will help you meet your quotas much faster.
- Prevent crazy-busy prospects, who sometimes get overwhelmed by the decision process, from staying with the status quo.

Finally, it's essential to realize that *you are the differentiator.* Not your product, service, or solution. You. That's why it's imperative to ensure you're leveraging strategies that will keep you at the top of your game.

> **GOAL:** Speed up your sales process,
> winning more deals along the way.

29.

TAP INTO TRIGGERS

QUIT WASTING YOUR PRECIOUS TIME ON THOSE SLOW-MOVING prospects who take an eternity to decide if it's worth it to make a change. They eat up way too many hours as well as a significant portion of your mental bandwidth.

You may not be aware of it, but there are organizations out there right now who have a tremendous need for your product or service. Actually, these potential clients aren't even thinking about buying anything yet. But something has happened that's altered their priorities. The change could be internal or external. Perhaps there's a newly emerging issue or competitor. Maybe they're going through a reorganization. Or they might be expanding rapidly.

This "trigger event" acts as a catalyst, forcing these organizations to reevaluate how they're doing things. Often, when seen through this new lens, their status quo is deemed insufficient to meet their changing objectives and requirements. At this point, the prospect may not be sure what to do. They just know that something has to change in the not-too-distant future.

For savvy sellers, this is the perfect time to get in touch with potential buyers. You can bring these companies ideas, insights, and information to help them deal with their emerging situation. According to Forrester Research, if you can create a viable vision for the future, you have a 74 percent chance of closing the sale. Not only is that an incredible close ratio, but these deals also move much faster than regular sales and you'll find yourself working against less competition.

If you know what these optimal trigger events are, you can pursue opportunities where you have this higher likelihood of closing an accelerated deal. Plus, you'll have the fodder you need for prospecting and having intelligent conversations with these prospects. Here's how to find and leverage these triggers for maximum impact at your company.

IDENTIFY THE TRIGGERS

Start by analyzing your existing client base, focusing first on internal factors. Think about what changes occurred within your clients' business that caused them to take action. Then consider external factors that may have changed the business environment significantly enough so that their status quo was no longer acceptable.

Often salespeople discover distinct changes or issues that are behind virtually all purchase decisions. Invariably, these are the common triggers:

- New leadership: Often, within three to six months, new executives implement fresh initiatives to drive revenue, reduce costs, or increase efficiencies.
- Financial announcements: If business is up, expansion projects take priority. If business is stagnant or down, productivity or cost-saving initiatives jump to the forefront.

- Mergers/acquisitions: Any change in this area prompts organizations to reevaluate all their supplier relationships.
- New strategic initiatives: When a new corporate directive is announced, the entire organization shifts to ensure alignment around this new direction.
- Legal/compliance: Changes in government regulations (ADA, FDA, OSHA, EPA) cause affected organizations to take immediate action.

These are only some of the many trigger events that can lead to accelerated sales possibilities. Others include new product/service announcements, relocations, market expansions, new business deals, or new funding.

If you're new to this type of thinking, review local or national business publications to identify potential triggers that could change an organization's priorities. For example, if you see that a technology company just received an infusion of $20 million in venture funding, ask yourself, "How could this impact that organization's need for what I sell?" The more you leverage trigger-event thinking, the more opportunities you'll find.

KEEPING UPDATED

Many of these trigger events are newsworthy announcements, shared publicly by the company. Or they're part of required financial reporting for public companies. The easiest way to get your hands on this info is to utilize sales intelligence tools—ones that automatically search for your specific catalysts and deliver them to you on a timely basis.

If you sell to a small number of companies or track a finite set of trigger events, you can get by with Google Alerts. Keeping updated this way becomes more complicated if you need a steady stream of new prospects, if you're selling to multiple market segments, or if a variety of these catalysts can signify a loosening of the status quo. That's when you need to use apps like InsideView, DiscoverOrg, or Lead411. They automate this tracking process for you, sorting through all the noise to find trigger events that meet your parameters and sending you daily alerts on what's happening in your territory. According to Aberdeen Group, 65 percent of best-in-class firms currently deploy formal trigger-event tools.

USING TRIGGERS

When you become aware of a trigger, it's time to initiate contact, via both e-mail and phone. Every single message you send should refer to the trigger event but in a slightly different way.

For example, if a company announces that third-quarter earnings were stagnant, here are several short messages you could send. Note how this one issue could impact virtually all areas within the organization.

> Alex, I see that [company name] just reported stagnant third-quarter earnings. Usually when that happens, everyone is chartered with finding ways to reduce costs or increase efficiencies. We've worked with a number of other organizations on this challenge. I have some ideas that may help you out. Can we set up a fifteen-minute conversation next Thursday afternoon to talk about them?

> Hi, Alex. I'm sure right now, with the recent earnings announcement, everyone is scrambling to find ways to drive costs out of their budgets. Sometimes it's hard to do when you think you're as efficient as you could possibly be. In our work with [similar

organization], we uncovered a way for them to cut an additional 7.2 percent on [savings area]. How does your calendar look on Tuesday morning?

Get the picture? When you tie the trigger event into the business outcomes that you deliver, suddenly you'll find yourself with interested prospects.

When you set up that initial meeting, make sure you talk about the trigger event, the challenges it creates for them, and their new objectives. Having an intelligent conversation around business issues is the first step in launching an accelerated sales cycle.

TRIGGER-EVENTS EXERCISE

Interview multiple clients who started using your product or service in the past six to twelve months. Ask them about what changed that suddenly made them decide it was time to do something different. If people initiate contact with your firm, ask them the same question. Your initial job is to determine what catalyzed the change initiative. Something did—or they would have stayed with the status quo.

For more info on trigger events, download the *Hidden Gems* e-book at www.jillkonrath.com/hidden-gems.

30.

DEVELOP TIME-SAVING SYSTEMS

WHEN I SPOKE WITH ALICIA, SHE'D JUST SPENT THE PAST twenty minutes trying to figure out what to write in a follow-up e-mail to a targeted prospect. She'd already reviewed her two previous messages, read her notes, and checked her contact's LinkedIn profile again.

No good ideas came to mind, so she sat there stuck. Finally, she sent a gracious "touching base" e-mail to her contact. With a big smile on her face, she checked it off her to-do list and moved on to the next prospect, repeating the exact same process.

What a colossal time suck! Yet it's exactly what most sellers do. Prospecting is typically treated as a one-off activity. Every attempt to reach a potential contact requires you to review, research, strategize, customize, and create a new outreach message. And since research from InsideSales.com shows that it can easily take eight to twelve attempts before you connect, we're talking about a lot of time invested to get in touch with just one person in one account. Multiply that by the number of prospects you're trying to reach and you'll see how quickly it adds up.

That's why it's imperative to view prospecting as a system, not a singular activity. You get much better results in less time when you approach it from this perspective. To think systematically about prospecting, consider these questions:

- Methods: How will you connect? Your options include e-mail, phone, voice mail, LinkedIn, Twitter, Facebook, networking events, and more.
- Message: What will you say in every contact? How can you create brief but relevant messages that pique curiosity and entice buyers to connect?
- Personalization: How can you easily customize your message? In what ways can you use social media to research, listen, and learn more about your buyers?
- Sequence: What's the best order in which to roll out your campaign? When is a good time to share info about helpful resources?

Yes, it's a lot of work up front. You have to create at least eight easily customizable messages that you can roll out over time. But the payback is huge. Because you're thinking strategically versus just reacting, you'll get better results with a systematized campaign.

I do a lot of work with midmarket sales organizations. My initial contact is usually the VP of sales. A typical campaign includes e-mail, voice mail, and social media outreach spread over a three-to-six-week period. Here's a sample campaign that I could use for targeted companies.

1. E-mail: Sales productivity is a hot issue these days. Everyone's trying to figure out which app is best. But technology isn't always the answer.

    Right now I'm helping [insert similar firms] give their sales-people an extra hour/day of selling time.

If that's of interest, let's set up a ten-minute call. How about next [weekday] at [time]?

2. Phone: Hi, [fill in name]. Jill Konrath here. I sent you an e-mail yesterday about how I'm helping increase sales productivity without adding new technology. I know that sounds impossible but it can be done.

    How does your calendar look for next [insert day] from 3 to 5 p.m.? Let me know. You can either RSVP to my e-mail or call me at [phone number].

3. LinkedIn: Go Bears! I didn't realize you were a big fan too. [Note: insert commonality.] As I mentioned in my previous messages, I work with sales organizations to help reps get lots more done in less time. And no, I'm not selling technology!

    If improving sales productivity is a major KPI this year, let's get some time on the calendar. I'm open next [insert day] afternoon.

4. E-mail: How can you get maximum productivity from your sales force? Even if you bring in tons of the coolest technology in the world, there's still the human factor to deal with.

    Here's an article from *HBR* on the high cost of distractions today: [www.insertlink.com]. Thought you'd find it interesting.

5. Phone: Hi, [fill in name]. Yesterday I sent you an article from *HBR* on the high cost of distractions. Believe it or not, distractions are actually costing your salespeople an hour or more every single day. But that's just one way your team is squandering their time. If you'd like to learn how I'm helping other sales teams, let's talk. I'm open on Friday morning. My number is [insert phone number].

6. E-mail: Most salespeople have absolutely no idea that the way they're working makes it harder for them to reach their numbers.

   If your sales kickoff is coming soon, perhaps it might make sense to bring in a speaker who can talk about increasing productivity in a motivating way. Here's a link to read more: [www.insert link.com].

   Let's set up a quick call to talk about what you're planning. Tuesday at 10:30?

   PS: If you're not the right person to talk to about your SKO, let me know whom I should contact instead.

7. LinkedIn: If you're planning your sales kickoff soon, you might want to consider focusing on helping your salespeople optimize their time. It's a huge issue.

   I've worked with [similar companies] this past year. If you're interested in what they had to say, check out their comments here: [www.insertlink.com].

   How about we pop on the phone for a ten-minute conversation? Would Monday at 10 a.m. ET work?

8. E-mail: Either you don't have a sales kickoff meeting coming soon, or you're not in charge of organizing it. Not to worry. I'll keep in touch until the time is right.

   In the meantime, I thought you might find this e-book helpful: *5 Strategies for Leading a Quota-Busting Sales Team*. [www .insertlink.com]. Enjoy!

There you have it. Eight messages planned in advance, ready to roll out with minimal effort to a targeted group of prospects who face similar challenges. Plus, your campaign can be amplified through

LinkedIn, Facebook, Twitter, and other social channels via commenting, sharing, or engaging in conversations. Think of all the time you can save by doing this systematically.

Another great application is creating a prospecting system to go after a targeted account—one that could have the potential for a big payoff if you landed it or expanded it. You often spend lots of time researching that one big account, learning about their business, strategic imperatives, competitive challenges, trigger events, and more. Once you've immersed yourself in all this, it's helpful to map out an eight-to-twelve-touch prospecting campaign that you can roll out over a two-to-three-week period.

Prospecting systems are just the start. How about referrals? Research shows that people are four times more likely to buy when referred by a friend (Nielsen). Additionally, they spend 13.2 percent more and have a 16 percent greater lifetime value than customers acquired through other methods (*Journal of Marketing*). Finally, they're a great way to get your messages returned. A referral from a trusted friend or colleague gives you immediate credibility, which frequently leads to significantly shorter sales cycles. What process can you create to ensure that you constantly ask for them?

Think about your proposals. Have you developed templates for frequently used information? Can you make your proposal templates easy to customize? Having a proposal system like this saves hours of time.

What about customer stories? While it's nice to have actual case studies written up, they're often difficult to obtain. But you can easily talk about similar customers facing similar challenges and the results they attained. Relating these real-life scenarios to your prospects helps them really understand the benefits of changing from the status quo. Rather than being haphazard about it, think about specific stories you can share based on the type of company you're talking to and the issues they're facing. Don't leave this to happenstance. If you do, under pressure your mind goes blank and you'll miss an opportunity to really stand out.

These are just thought starters. Just remember that systems trump activities all the time. Yes, they require forethought. Yes, you'll end up tinkering with them as you learn more about what works well and what needs to be changed. In the end, however, they'll save you time and energy as you focus on bigger and better targets.

SYSTEMATIZE-IT EXERCISE

Choose a common issue faced by your prospects that's solvable by your product or service. Identify likely buyers (by position) who are involved in the decision. Then, take some time to immerse yourself in understanding their responsibilities, objectives, challenges, initiatives, and more. To help with this, download the Buyers Matrix, a tool that I've previously written about in *SNAP Selling* and *Agile Selling*: www.jillkonrath.com/buyers-matrix.

When you're ready, plot out an entire eight-touch campaign that you can use to set up meetings with these prospects. Roll it out on just a few prospects first to see how it works, then make adjustments to improve it.

31.

UNCLOG YOUR PIPELINE

THE LAST THING YOU WANT TO DO IS WASTE YOUR PRECIOUS time on prospects who aren't going to close. I'm talking about accounts that aren't budging, even though you think your solution would be great for them. After a barrage of "checking in" and "touching base" messages, you're stymied about what to do next.

Recently I sat down with Trey, who sells marketing research services, to talk about his overflowing pipeline. He'd been working at the company for 2.5 years and was proud of all the prospects he'd developed during that time frame. As we went through them one by one, I'd ask these questions:

- Have they decided to change or are they still trying to determine if it makes sense?
- What business value will they realize if they decide to go ahead?
- What's the next step? What specifically is your prospect doing to advance their buying process? What are you doing?

Trey's most frequent responses were "Well, they like our solution a lot" or "They told me to keep in touch." In most cases, he couldn't articulate the value these "stuck" prospects would realize if they'd change. In short, if there was a compelling need, a strong business case, or even a trigger that could create urgency, Trey couldn't identify it. But he was still confident they would close in the not-too-distant future— or at least he hoped they would.

WHY DEALS GET STUCK

Bulging pipelines fool even the best salespeople, keeping them from pursuing new and better opportunities. It's imperative to either purge these time sinkholes or get them moving again. Here are the most common reasons why deals get stuck and ideas on how to address them.

Don't See Enough Value

Buyers disappear if they don't feel that the business case justifies the effort to change from the status quo. It's simply easier to stay with what they're doing today. To prevent this, invest more time up front on the buyer's issues, challenges, and objectives. Discuss the full value of your offering as it relates to their organization. Make it personal.

To reignite clogged opportunities, refocus on the business case. Share case studies, cite research, connect them with clients, suggest an assessment, raise the cost of delayed action, or point out the opportunity cost.

More Important Priorities

Sometimes when prospects tell you that other priorities take precedence, it's 100 percent true. You just have to wait for better timing. To keep in the game though, find out what their top priorities are right now. Then, step back and try to "connect the dots" between your prospects' business priorities and what you sell.

For example, when oil and gas prices recently plummeted, buyers in that industry went into shock. Budgets were slashed, decisions delayed. To unclog stuck deals, I helped one client's salespeople align with buyers with the following message: "With oil prices down, I know there's tons of uncertainty right now regarding the future. That's actually why we need to talk again. You need to increase efficiency—now, not in six months—and I've got some ideas for you." With this message, many prospects reengaged.

Wrong Person

You finally reach someone who's interested in learning more within the prospect organization. This person asks lots of question, likes talking to you, and even requests more information. Yet all too often, that's as far as it goes. They lack the power and drive to lead a change initiative in their organization.

The issue here is that you've placed all your bets on one person. Yet according to research from CEB, most decisions today involve 5.4 individuals. To get this prospect moving again, you'll need to initiate contact with more people in the account beyond your one contact. Think about which "positions" typically weigh in on decisions related to your product or service and use LinkedIn to find out who those individuals are in the prospect company.

At the same time, you should let your primary contact know that when companies make buying decisions about your offering, typically these other "positions" are involved in the process. Then, inform your contact that you plan to get in touch with these other people in the upcoming weeks to get their input—and that you'll be getting back to him or her shortly.

Misjudged Interest

It's so easy to misinterpret polite interest as serious consideration. Unfortunately, wishful thinking does not lead to signed deals. In this situation, there's only one thing we can do: learn to ask tougher questions. There's no use wasting time on nice prospects who'll never budge. We need to ask:

- If you stay with your status quo, will you be able to meet your objectives?
- How big of an issue is the one you described? What else does it impact?
- From your perspective, what's the value of changing? Can you be more explicit?
- Of all your primary initiatives, where does something like this rank—and why?

Honest conversations help you and your prospect determine if it's worth it to keep talking. Some will reengage with you because there's a strong business reason to do so. Others will disqualify themselves. At least you'll know.

No Reason

If you've already given your prospect everything they need, they have no reason to talk with you unless they decide to take action. That could take an eternity, so it's up to you to come up with a valid reason for another conversation. Put on your thinking cap and explore these categories to figure one out:

- Fresh perspectives: What additional ideas, insights, and information can you share about the business case, implementation, decision consideration, other clients, and so forth?
- Blind spots: What might they not be thinking of that they should be considering?
- Hot topics: Are there any recent trigger events occurring within or outside their organization that could impact their decision?

Unclogging your pipeline requires creativity and additional research. It's hard for prospects to ignore it when you contact them with messages like, "I've been thinking about our last conversation and have an idea to help you achieve your objectives faster. Do you have fifteen minutes for a quick conversation next week?"

FLUSH 'EM OUT

Initially Trey was reluctant to use the above strategies. Knowing the truth about where your "hot prospects" really stand can be scary. Humbling too when you realize that you've been deluding yourself. But over the course of thirty days, Trey reinitiated contact with nearly all of them. He had many honest conversations, shared numerous fresh ideas, and expanded his contacts in many accounts.

As a result, he flushed many of these prospects out of his pipeline. While still in his CRM, they weren't active, although he did plan to reconnect with many of them in four to five months. Believe it or not, Trey felt relieved not having to constantly stress out about them. He also reignited a number of other languishing opportunities and closed some nice-sized deals.

It's time to stop "circling back" with slow-moving prospects. Be strategic about keeping them moving—or move them out.

UNCLOGGED EXPERIMENT

Pick ten accounts in your pipeline that *should* have closed by now but haven't. Decide which of the above approaches would work best for each opportunity and take the appropriate action. When you leave messages, focus on piquing curiosity enough to engage buyers in a short conversation so you can make a decision whether to keep pursuing them or not. Used effectively, many of these strategies can significantly accelerate the sales process. If they don't, it's okay to remove these prospects from your pipeline.

32.

CREATE AN UPWARD SPIRAL

WHAT'S GETTING IN THE WAY OF ACHIEVING—OR EVEN overachieving—your sales goals? When I ask sellers this question, I frequently hear comments like these: their prospects are happy with their current provider, they believe it's too big a hassle to change, they think the price is too high, or they just don't get it. Or they complain about a lack of training, a bad boss, or impossible-to-reach quotas. They criticize people on their own team for not getting back to them on a timely basis.

The finger is nearly always pointed "out there" at some amorphous object or immovable obstacle. But the reality is much closer to home. While we can't change our prospects, we can change ourselves. We have 100 percent control over what we say and do.

Once we grasp this, we have an immense opportunity to create an upward spiral, enabling us to close more sales in less time. To do so, we need to become our own best coaches—a strategy that top sellers use all the time. Their focus is on effectiveness and "getting better," which is the flip side of efficiency.

Use this process to accelerate your upward spiral—one that ensures that you continually upgrade and build on your knowledge, skills, and experience.

1. GET CURIOUS

When things don't work out, open yourself to the possibility that perhaps if you'd done something different, you might have gotten a different outcome. For example, if prospects:

- Don't respond to your voice mail or e-mail messages, what changes could you make to your messaging?
- Keep giving you the same objections, what might you be saying that creates them?
- Don't want to engage after an initial conversation, what would it take to get them more interested?
- Tell you that they've decided to stick with the status quo, how could you better help them realize the value of making a change?
- Choose to do business with your competitor, what do you need to know or do differently to ensure it doesn't happen again?

Getting curious is the best way to get the improvement engine in gear. It starts the search for more effective ways of selling.

2. GET SMARTER

Once you've identified an area you want to improve in, immerse yourself in studying how to be more effective. Start with your colleagues. Find out what they're doing that's working. Ask how they've dealt with the tough situations you're facing. Study what sales experts are saying. There's a wealth of great information online that can help. Read sales books too—their in-depth approach enables you to see how the entire process works, versus just the one technique or tactic that's covered in a typical blog post.

As part of your immersion, think about whether your problem is a root cause or a symptom. For example, if you have trouble closing deals, it's probably because prospects don't see enough value in changing. Working on your closing skills won't solve the problem.

3. EXPERIMENT

Yes, we're back to that again. Throughout this book, I've repeatedly challenged you to try new things and create your own experiments. For example, if you use PowerPoint slides at some point in the sales process, try going without. Or try fewer slides or mixing up the order. Your goal is to increase your effectiveness. Unless you experiment with new approaches, you won't know what's even possible.

Before you go "live" with real clients, step back and analyze what you're doing from your prospect's perspective. Using the "as if" strategy, put yourself in the mind frame of your targeted buyer. Then, take a look at your new approach "as if" you were that person. Ask questions like: Does it pique your interest? Inspire you to change? Remove objections? If it doesn't, change things up and do it again.

Also, if it's possible with your specific experiment, record yourself. Seeing your presentation on video or listening to a recent phone conversation can give you invaluable insights on what you missed and how you might improve.

4. GET FEEDBACK

Self-assessment is great, but it can only take you so far. Getting other people's perspectives can take you to another level. Share your approaches with your colleagues or boss and invite feedback: What did they like? What didn't work well? What suggestions do they have for improvement? If possible, create a mock-meeting scenario so that you can run through an entire conversation. While role-playing feels awkward, it's a great way to get better.

5. CHALLENGE YOURSELF

Using a CRM system, you can easily track metrics such as how many e-mail/phone "touches" it took before you connected with a prospect, how many initial conversations led to follow-up meetings, and how many prospects stayed with their status quo instead of changing. This is invaluable data. It also gives you a way to compare the effectiveness of your new approaches with your historical data.

Give yourself specific goals. See if you can connect with prospects in fewer touches or if you can reduce your losses to no-decision. Make it a game, tracking your progress.

Keep at it too. Learners don't develop proficiency overnight. New approaches feel awkward at first. You stumble over your own words. They're not one bit natural. But if your ultimate goal is to sell more in less time, increasing your sales effectiveness goes a long way toward achieving it.

EYE-OPENER EXPERIMENT

Next time you're tempted to blame external factors for things being tough, take a look at your own possible complicity in the situation. Get curious and ask yourself questions like these: Where exactly did I run into problems? What could I have done differently? At this point, your challenge is to identify at least ten different things you could have done. Get input from your colleagues. Check out what sales experts recommend. Don't let yourself off easy! There are always ways to improve your sales skills.

33.

MAKE DECISIONS SIMPLER

YOUR PROSPECTS ARE CRAZY BUSY TOO. THEIR CALENDARS are overflowing, they're constantly falling behind, and they feel powerless to stop the unrelenting, escalating demands on their time (sound familiar?). When people are overwhelmed, complexity of any sort brings their production to a screeching halt.

As a seller, you introduce additional complexity into your prospects' lives. Making a decision to engage with you and consider changing from the status quo is difficult. Today's buying team typically includes five people, all of whom have different (or even competing) needs, interests, and issues. They may even be dispersed across the country or globally. Getting them to agree on anything is a huge challenge. Matters are further complicated because your prospects don't make these kinds of decisions on a regular basis. Making a bad choice can be career derailing.

That's why, according to CEB, many change initiatives are abandoned only 37 percent of the way through the decision process, even though the company could really benefit from seeing them through.

It's just too hard. There's only one thing you can do to remedy this situation—make the decision easier for your prospect.

These strategies can help you get through to overwhelmed buyers:

OUTLINE THE ROAD MAP

To get things moving, your initial step is to pique your prospect's curiosity about the value of making the change. They need to believe it's sufficient to warrant an investment of time and effort. Once they agree your proposition is worthy of further investigation, show them a road map of how companies typically make these types of decisions.

Think of yourself as a project manager who's explaining the major project steps—not in excruciating detail but as a high-level overview. Help the buyer understand who needs to be involved and why. Show them what you'll be doing with them, as well as the steps they'll need to go through themselves as they move along the decision path. Talk about time frames, working backward from when they'd like to be operational.

This is not selling; this is simplifying. If, after going through all this, the prospect decides it's too much for right now, you'll know soon, without wasting any more time.

TALK ABOUT TOUGH STUFF

Hope doesn't help you sell more in less time. Candid conversations do. You need to address potential issues up front—unflinchingly.

There have been times when I've been sick to my stomach asking questions like these:

- Based on your objectives, why do you feel that changing from the status quo is a necessary imperative?

- What will it realistically take to get a project like this funded?
- Who's not going to be happy with this change initiative and why?
- What are the drawbacks of making a change?

By talking about these matters openly, you're seen as an ally or a consultant, not another self-serving salesperson. Plus, it helps you and your primary contact(s) plan a path forward that addresses or eliminates possible show-stopping obstacles.

START SMALLER

Sometimes, in talking to prospects, you uncover so many opportunities for your products or services that you start to drool. You picture yourself signing a massive contract that literally makes your year. In fact, you can't imagine a better way to sell more in less time.

In reality, however, the bigger a decision, the longer it typically takes to get approval. During that time frame, so many things can go wrong—a bad third quarter, a change in leadership, or a new competitive offering. Unless you're selling an enterprise solution, you'd be much smarter to get started with a smaller deal than risk losing it entirely.

Propose an initial assessment to better understand the scope of the problem. Tackle a small issue so you can demonstrate immediate results. Focus on only one of your products or services, not the whole shebang. Suggest a change in only one area of the company to test viability before rolling it out everywhere. The key is to get your foot in the door, prove your worth, build relationships, and then expand.

CREATE TOOLS

One of the best ways to make decisions simpler is to develop tools to help prospects through challenging parts of the buying process. For people who have a tough time justifying the business case, put together an easy-to-use template in which they can fill in their own data. Create ROI tools they can use to quickly figure out how soon the investment will pay for itself. Develop checklists to ensure prospects don't miss any key steps in their decision process. Put together a competitive assessment tool to help them evaluate the different vendors, making sure to include your core strengths.

Make *simple* your buzzword. In a chaotic, constantly changing business environment, it's a huge factor for winning deals with the overwhelmed buyer. Most sales organizations don't realize that, which can give you a massive competitive advantage.

SIMPLIFY-IT EXPERIMENT

Take a serious look at your own sales process. At what points do your prospects run into obstacles? Do they have trouble justifying change? Is it hard to evaluate their options? Do they get confused about what to do next? Play around with creating a simple tool you can use to make the decision process easier for them. Test it, fine-tune it, and then share it with colleagues.

PS: For more ideas on selling to crazy-busy buyers, read *SNAP Selling: Speed Up Sales and Win More Business with Today's Frazzled Customers.*

34.

GET BIGGER CLIENTS

IF YOU WORK FOR A SMALL COMPANY OR ARE AN INDEPEN-
dent professional, this message is specifically for you. There's nothing tougher than selling to other microbusinesses, even if they have a tremendous need for your product or services.

First off, many of them are real penny-pinchers; they have to be. By targeting these companies, you immediately limit your income potential. To compensate for the low dollar value of each client, you need to spend more much more time on sales-related activities. There might not be enough hours in the day to earn a decent living.

If you sell services, you run into another problem. Smaller clients lack knowledge about what it takes to do your job. In retrospect, I pity my first website designer, Andrew. He was just starting up and needed references and money, but working with me turned out to be a difficult challenge. I constantly changed my mind. I questioned his judgment. I'd come up with "brilliant" ideas that turned out to be a nightmare to implement. Occasionally he'd want to charge an additional fee but I'd get upset when I found out how much extra it was.

As the project progressed, he felt grossly undervalued because he was doing so much unpaid extra work. I also undermined his confidence that he could build a profitable business. I wasn't trying to be a jerk. I was simply clueless about how much work went into building a website. In short, I was a terrible time suck and a grossly unprofitable client.

That doesn't happen if you sell to bigger companies. They expect to pay higher rates for services. After all, it's a sign of your competence. There's already money in the budget that, with the right business case, could be allocated to you. Even better, once you land an initial contract, it's much easier to get add-on sales in other divisions or business units.

REVENUE LADDER

Many entrepreneurs think it's imperative to first achieve success with microbusinesses before moving on to bigger clients. Unfortunately, many never get the opportunity to move up into bigger sales. They wind up working too darn hard for the amount of revenue coming in. Ultimately, these aspiring entrepreneurs shut their business down and go find themselves a job that's not quite as difficult.

To make more sales in less time, you need to call on bigger organizations. Please note that I'm not advising you to call on global giants right away. They won't be interested in you unless you have a unique expertise or come from the corporate environment.

Instead, you can move upmarket to slightly bigger firms than the ones you work with today. If you currently sell to companies with revenues of:

- $1 million or less, pursue organizations with $5 million to $10 million in revenue;

- $1 million to $25 million, raise your sights to companies with $50 million in revenue;
- $25 million to $50 million, go after firms with $100 million in revenue;
- $50 million to $100 million, target $500 million firms or business units in big companies.

Challenge yourself to work your way up the revenue ladder. By moving up rung by rung, you develop the confidence, expertise, and referral accounts needed to sell at the next level.

WHAT BIGGER COMPANIES EXPECT

Pursuing business with larger organizations requires you to step up your game too. With every decision involving multiple people, it often takes several months (or longer) to close a deal. Expect to have numerous meetings from the onset and make sure you plan well for them.

Your first conversation needs to focus on issues and challenges that are relevant to your prospect's objectives and addressable by your offering. Corporate decision makers have zero tolerance for product-pushing peddlers. Zero. If you pitch them in an e-mail, voice mail, phone call, or meeting, they will delete or dismiss you in a nanosecond. They hate pitches with a passion. From their perspective, it is an insult and a total waste of their time.

In *Selling to Big Companies*, I spell out numerous strategies for getting your foot in the door of these larger organizations. To be successful, go slower and strategize more. Make sure to invest time doing the following:

- **Researching.** This is literally the price of admission. Unless you invest time learning about their organization, business drivers, and challenges, you won't have a chance. Review their website and check out the latest news. Then hop over to LinkedIn to identify people to contact, making sure to read their profiles. They expect you to know this information *before* you meet.

- **Prepping.** Now that you have this info, figure out how to best leverage it to launch an eight-to-ten-touch campaign (via e-mail/ phone/LinkedIn) to set up a meeting. Again, never pitch. Your initial goal is simply to pique curiosity about how you can help them address a business issue. Practice calling yourself and leaving a message. After listening to it, make it better—and probably shorter. Same with e-mails. Make them short, sweet, and to the point.

When you get a meeting set up, plan for that too, more than you've ever planned before. Figure out a short introduction, which highlights your business case. Figure out eight to ten questions to help you get an initial feel for their priorities, status quo, and objectives relevant to your offering. Determine a realistic, logical next step. Run through the entire meeting in your mind. Then do a mock meeting with a colleague playing the role of your prospect. Find any glitches and adjust your plan accordingly.

Every time you take a step up the ladder, there's a lot more at stake. But it's so worth it. Imagine making an initial sell of $10,000 to a bigger company. Assuming people are satisfied with your product or service, you now have an excellent opportunity to expand your presence in this account. And with an internal referral, the second, third, and other future sales are a whole lot easier and more profitable.

UP-YOUR-ANTE EXPERIMENT

Identify ten organizations that are bigger than your current customers and, based on your best guess, could benefit from your product or service. Research them to get a good sense of what they do, how you might help, and whom you'd connect with.

After going through the first part of this exercise, pick the company you'd *least* like to work with. At first it's highly likely you're going to make some serious sales-blowing mistakes; virtually everyone does. That's why you don't go after your most desirable accounts right away.

Approach this first company to practice what you say, how you say it, and how it flows. Pay particular attention to the objections and obstacles you run into. Afterward try to figure out how to avoid these stuck points or better deal with them in the future.

KEY POINTS:
ACCELERATE SALES

- Leverage trigger events to identify accounts who have a high propensity to change in the not-too-distant future. If you get in early, you can set the buying vision—and achieve an unbelievable 74 percent close rate.

- Think systems, not activities. Any time you catch yourself doing repetitive work, think, *How can I systematize this? Can I create an easily customizable template?* Creating systems reduces thinking and planning time and increases sales effectiveness. Good places to start include prospecting, proposals, presentations, and referrals.

- Don't let sluggish deals clog up your pipeline. Keep them moving by reigniting their focus on the business case, expanding your contacts, and tying your offering into their main priorities. Stay in touch by offering fresh perspectives, insights into blind spots, and updated info on emerging topics.

- Get curious (not upset) when you run into tough sales problems. They're growth opportunities in disguise. Immerse yourself in learning new strategies to deal with them. Challenge yourself to get to the next level!

- Simplify, simplify, simplify. Today's crazy-busy buyers can't handle complexity. Outline the decision road map. Talk about the tough stuff. Make it so easy to say yes that they can't refuse. Whenever possible, create tools to help guide your prospects and keep them moving.
- Pursue business with bigger companies. Not only will this provide larger deals, but you can also sell to other business units and departments once you establish yourself as a viable vendor. You'll spend less time prospecting and more time on account growth. Every add-on deal will be significantly more profitable.

Download the Accelerate Sales Summary PDF at www.jillkonrath.com/accelerate-sales-pdf.

PART 7
FINAL WORDS

35.

WRAPPING IT UP

NO ONE EVER PREPARED US FOR THIS "AGE OF DISTRACTION." On one hand, it's exhilarating to have all this information at our fingertips. We can find out so much about our prospects before we even make contact. We can communicate via e-mail, LinkedIn, Twitter, and other social media channels.

But if we're not careful, we get lured into a web of interruptions and distractions, spending hours clicking around on various websites, articles, and apps—taking us away from our real work.

So we put in more hours and check e-mail more often. And every little decision erodes our mental capacity, making it tougher to come up with fresh strategies or learn new things.

Ultimately, we move into "overwhelm" mode. We tell ourselves that being busy is good for our career or that it's what you have to do to get ahead today. Yet we dream of taking a long vacation and never coming back.

That's where I was when I started this quest. I was sick and tired of being crazy busy. I felt like my life was spinning out of control. I didn't think there was anything I could do about it—except work even harder or longer hours.

When I finally took back control of my life, I was astounded at how much work I could get done in a concentrated period of time. I freed up hours each week. The best part was that the quality of my work improved dramatically. With more time, I prepared better for my client meetings. I was more strategic, which increased my effectiveness.

Have I achieved my goal of maintaining my income while working thirty-six hours per week? Not quite yet. It's an ambitious goal and I knew it would take a while to get there. But I am well on my way. Freeing up more time on my calendar allowed my creativity to blossom too. Right now I'm exploring some new ways to drive revenue that weren't even figments of my imagination when I began this quest. The future looks bright.

KISS CRAZY BUSY GOOD-BYE

Today, when people ask how things are going, I no longer tell them I'm crazy busy. I am so done with that lifestyle. Crazy busy is not correlated with optimal productivity. Nor is it a badge of honor. Instead, I say, "I'm great—working less and doing more."

Now let's talk about you. You can change your life too. After fighting (and overcoming) the crazy-busy battle for eight years, I'm confident of that. Since we are, by nature, eminently susceptible to distractions, I'd encourage you to focus on reducing their impact immediately. Right now they're costing you at least one to two hours per day, time that could be much better spent prepping for or working with potential buyers.

The other reason to start here and now is directly related to business commerce. Savvy marketers invest tremendous sums of money and time studying how to tempt you into their world. They try different messaging, mediums, colors, and noises to capture your attention and get you to click. They design addictive apps, games, and products to keep you engaged while they gather even more data about you, which they either sell or use to further lure you in.

The "pull" is going to get worse. Either we're going to be putty in these marketers' hands, doing whatever they want us to do, or we're going to make our own decisions about where and how we invest our time. The sooner we learn how to do this, the better.

When you figure out how to optimize your work and minimize distractions, you become significantly more productive, your sales skills improve, and your knowledge grows, constantly. In short, you turn yourself into an invaluable asset—so much so that *you* become the differentiator instead of your products or services.

WORDS OF WISDOM

If you've made it this far, you're obviously committed to making changes that will enable you to sell more in less time. Bravo! It can be done. Here are my final thoughts on making it work for you.

- Start small. Even though you're likely an overachiever, if you try to change too much too quickly, you'll set yourself up for failure. Begin with one hour, one day, or one activity at a time—and build up.
- Be an experimenter. Try things out, testing new ways. Be curious about what you learn. There's no right or wrong, only interesting observations. If you like the results, incorporate the new approach into how you work.
- Take good care of yourself. Working all the time isn't good for you physically, mentally, or socially. To do your best work, you need sleep, fun, relationships, and movement.

- Play with change. Don't make it onerous. Don't get into a head-to-head battle with your bad habits. Have some fun. While you may laugh at the Time Master, it enabled me to effortlessly incorporate new behaviors.
- Engage others. You're not the only one with these challenges. Invite some friends or colleagues to try these ideas with you. Compare results, share ideas, and be a little competitive.

Most of all, keep at it. It's taken you years to develop your daily work habits and they won't change overnight. When you do screw up, which you invariably will, restart the process and keep on going. Slowly, but surely, over the course of a year, I optimized myself. Today, I'm having the time of my life and enjoying sales more than ever—and I wish the same for you.

APPENDIX 1: LEADING A HIGHLY PRODUCTIVE SALES TEAM

As a sales leader, increasing your team's productivity is one of your biggest challenges. Growing revenue without adding salespeople can seem like an insurmountable task. However, there are a whole slew of actions you can take to give your reps more customer-facing time.

Research by Pace Productivity shows that only 22 percent of a salesperson's time is spent on sales activities such as prepping, conversations, and meetings. Assuming a 40-hour week, that equates to 8.8 hours. At the same time, VoloMetrix reports that top sellers spend 33 percent more time with customers, which is less than three additional hours a week.

When viewed that way, your challenge becomes manageable. You don't need to hire more people. Instead, you need to help your team rescue time lost to distractions. You need to help them optimize their workday so they're spending more time on work that matters.

Dictating "Thou shalt work harder on more important things" isn't the answer. Your already-overwhelmed reps will think you're crazy. To the best of their knowledge, they're working as hard as they can; they don't know any other way to do their job.

Before jumping in with any quick fixes or radical suggestions, first observe your sales team in action. How are they spending their time? Are they constantly switching from task to task? How long does it take them to respond to one of your e-mails? Are they spending enough time prepping for important conversations? It's highly likely that some of your team members are significantly more productive than others. Notice what they're doing differently.

Talk to your reps about what you're doing. Let them know you're not policing them but trying to figure out ways to help them sell more in less time so they can be more successful. It's essential to frame things from this perspective. Your team needs to know you care about them first and foremost. Also, if your reps feel like they're being judged, implementing any changes will be much tougher.

Observe yourself too. You'll likely find you have lots of opportunities for improvement. Let your sales team know what you've discovered in your own self-assessment. The reality is, you're all in this together.

Use the following strategies to help you and your team close more deals in less time.

EXPAND THE KNOWLEDGE BASE

Virtually every change initiative begins with knowing that a better way exists. Right now, few of your salespeople will have focused on their personal productivity. They will have minimal knowledge about how their daily habits and distractions negatively impact their sales success. They inadvertently work on less important tasks first.

Start by helping reps recognize the value of their time. Share information about recent research, sales hacks, optimizing their day, and getting more done. Forward interesting articles to your reps with a quick note on why they're important or interesting. Give your team copies of this book. Attend webinars with a "sell more in less time" emphasis.

Use team meetings to further the learning. Initiate conversations about what reps (and you) are observing and learning regarding their behaviors. Assign reps different topics to teach their colleagues at upcoming lunch and learns. More than anything, remember that this is in the spirit of helping your sales team be more successful.

MAKE IT A CHALLENGE

Challenges engage us. They invite us to try new approaches and to stretch out of our comfort zone.

One of the best ways to begin is by challenging your sales reps to figure out how they're really spending their own time. Encourage them to use a tool like RescueTime (and pay for it if you can). Share with them what they might learn by conducting a self-analysis like this. But importantly, don't force reps to share results with you or they'll feel like you're Big Brother. Instead, ask them to use what they've learned to start conversations on how they can get better.

In this book, you'll find dozens of productivity experiments you can use as individual or team challenges. Do them with your team. Encourage reps to challenge each other to get better. Turn some into contests to see who gets the best results. Make sure to participate yourself.

BECOME A TIME PROTECTOR

As a sales leader, your primary focus should be on protecting your reps' time. Just by doing this, you can add hours to their workday.

Create "power hours." Have your reps set aside one hour in the morning and one in the afternoon where they focus 100 percent on one high-value activity. Many sales organizations devote one of these sixty-minute segments entirely to outbound phone calling. Not researching. Not prepping. Just calling. Spending a full hour on any one task (writing proposals, strategizing on accounts) significantly increases the quality of a person's thinking as well as the amount of work that gets done.

Establish rules. Having "how we work" rules gets more of your reps doing the right stuff more often. Here are some good rules you can implement.

- Take ten minutes at the start of the day to identify your top three priorities.
- Schedule your day/tasks before you begin.
- Check your e-mail at 8:30, 10:00, 11:30, 1:00, 2:30, and 4:00.
- Take a fifteen-minute break every ninety minutes. Get away from your desk.

This can be extremely helpful for new hires, as you'll get them set up for success from the get-go.

Get rid of time sucks and unnecessary interruptions. Keep a constant lookout for tasks like contract approvals, scheduling, and customer service issues that eat up your reps' time. Look for alternate and cost-efficient ways to handle these issues.

By the way, this includes you too. Don't expect your reps to stop everything they're doing to get back to you in ten minutes. For example, on the fifteenth of each month, many sales leaders panic when it looks like they might not meet their forecast. They request immediate updates on all unclosed accounts. To prevent knee-jerk reactions like this, put a system in place to request this info the day before, always.

ESCALATE THE UPWARD SPIRAL

A continuous focus on helping your reps improve their sales skills is absolutely essential. Encourage them to get curious about areas where they need improvement. Help them learn what they need to in order to be better at their jobs. Role-play with them and conduct mock meetings.

Here's a bit of heresy for you. For decades, sales organizations have tracked metrics such as calls per day, meetings scheduled, demos given, and proposals delivered as well as conversion rates for everything. Every rep is expected to abide by these one-size-fits-all standards. But since salespeople have wildly different experience and skill levels, these often turn out to be bogus measurements.

To really help your reps get better, focus on customized metrics for each person. With newer salespeople, direct them to the specific metric they need to improve, such as initial call or demo conversion rates. For more experienced reps, have a genuine conversation regarding the area they see as their biggest challenge. Encourage them to learn from their peers, industry experts, and their customers.

Check out programs to help yourself in this area too. Companies like ExecVision.io record phone calls and enable reps/teams to listen to themselves and others. They can get and give feedback about their performance, thus upping everyone's skill level.

LEVERAGE SALES-ACCELERATION TOOLS

While this book focuses on the human side of sales productivity, keeping up-to-date on emerging technologies is essential for increasing sales productivity. Always be thinking, *How can I free up more of my salespeople's time so that they can spend more time on the right customer-facing activities?*

In addition to having a decent CRM system, make sure to evaluate if these tools can help your team:

- Sales intelligence tools to build prospecting lists, find out how to connect, and discover invaluable insights about people/companies. (LinkedIn, InsideView, DiscoverOrg, and Charlie App)
- E-mail engagement tools to inform when sent e-mails are read and forwarded, when attachments are opened, and more. Plus, you can create e-mail templates and automate sequences. (HubSpot Sales, ClearSlide, LiveHive, Yesware, ToutApp)
- Online meetings technology to enable remote reps to have in-person meetings, build relationships, and speed up the sales process. Today's buyers often prefer these meetings. (GoToMeeting, join.me, and Zoom.us)
- Inside-sales/lead-generation technologies like power dialers, intelligent lead distribution, sales workflow, and prioritization to quickly turn more leads into revenue. (Velocify, InsideSales.com)
- Team messaging. If internal team or company conversations clog up your in-box, use a team collaboration tool to simplify things. (Slack)

There are tons of technologies out there, a panacea of solutions. Pick one, implement it, and make it successful first before you introduce others. Most importantly, don't be penny-wise and pound-foolish.

FINALLY . . .

Become a role model yourself. How you work matters. Your behavior sets a precedent for your entire team. If you're feeling overwhelmed and constantly telling people how crazy busy you are, it's highly likely your whole team is facing a whirlwind of distraction too.

Take a deep breath, dig in, and start incorporating the suggestions in this book. It's not easy, but it does make a big difference. Instead of bouncing off the walls with the zillion things you need to do, you'll be focused on what really matters.

At first, it's a real challenge. You'll definitely have empathy for what your team is going through too. That's a good thing. You can talk about it and grow together. Ultimately, you'll all sell more in less time!

APPENDIX 2: KEEP ON LEARNING

If you want to dig deeper, you'll love these excellent and interesting resources featuring many of the experts whose work I cited in this book. Watching or listening to them can be a great break for you, especially after a period of intense focus.

TED TALKS

"How to Stay Calm When You Know You'll Be Stressed" (12 minutes): Neuroscientist Daniel Levitin shares how to use premortems to handle tough situations that can hijack your brain. http://bit.ly/calm-stress.

"What Makes Some Technology so Habit-Forming?" (13 minutes): Nir Eyal, the "Prophet of Habit-Forming Technology," shares how technology companies design products we can't put down. http://bit.ly/habit-forming.

"Forget Big Change, Start with a Tiny Habit" (17 minutes): Behavior scientist B. J. Fogg explains the value of tiny habits in changing behavior one small step at a time. http://bit.ly/tiny-tiny-habits.

"A Simple Way to Break a Bad Habit" (9 minutes): Psychiatrist Judson Brewer shares how being curious transforms how we think about our bad habits. http://bit.ly/stop-bad-habits.

"The Happy Secret to Better Work" (12 minutes): Psychologist Shawn Achor answers the question, "Which comes first, happiness or better work?" and what we can do about it. http://bit.ly/happiness-work.

"Your Body Language Shapes Who You Are" (21 minutes): Social psychologist Amy Cuddy shows how changing our posture changes us. http://bit.ly/cuddy-TED-talk.

"One More Reason to Get a Good Night's Sleep" (11 minutes): Neuroscientist Jeff Iliff shares what's actually going on in your brain when you're sleeping. http://bit.ly/sleeping-brain.

"Why Do We Sleep?" (21 minutes): Circadian neuroscientist Russell Foster studies the sleep cycles of our brains and the impact they have on us during the daytime. http://bit.ly/brain-asleep.

"Got a Meeting? Take a Walk" (4 minutes): Business innovator Nilofer Merchant suggests a small idea that just might have a big impact on your life and health. http://bit.ly/walk-walk.

"Play Is More than Just Fun" (26 minutes): Dr. Stuart Brown, founder of the National Institute for Play, shares research on why play makes us smarter at every age. http://bit.ly/play-is-more-than-fun.

VIDEOS

"The Backwards Brain Bicycle" (8 minutes): Consulting engineer Destin Sandlin shows why it's so hard to learn something new. http://bit.ly/backward-bike.

"The As If Principle" (1.5 minutes): In this mini video, psychologist Richard Wiseman shares numerous ways that small actions can transform our lives. http://bit.ly/as-if.

"The Pomodoro Technique" (5 minutes): Marketing consultant Greg Head shares how to use short bursts of intense concentration in the midst of your busy life. http://bit.ly/try-a-pomodoro.

"Track Your Small Wins to Motivate Big Accomplishments" (21 minutes): Harvard professor Teresa Amabile shares a five-minute daily strategy to keep you motivated at work. http://bit.ly/small-wins-motivate.

"The 4 Ways to Successfully Adopt New Habits" (18 minutes): Best-selling author Gretchen Rubin shares four tendencies that impact how we pick up new habits. http://bit.ly/adopt-new-habits.

"The Willpower Instinct" (54 minutes): Health psychologist Kelly McGonigal shares research on how to resist temptation, stop procrastinating, and fulfill your long-term goals. http://bit.ly/more-willpower.

"Fearless Leadership: From Politics to the Boardroom" (47 minutes): In this keynote, publisher Arianna Huffington talks about what we need to do to thrive in today's busy world. http://bit.ly/success-sleep.

ONLINE RESOURCES

"Quiz: The Four Tendencies": Take this free assessment, based on Gretchen Rubin's book *Better than Before*, to discover your primary tendency and strategies to maximize it. http://bit.ly/four-tendencies.

"Procrastination Survey": Find out your procrastination profile and get a few scientifically proven tips for taming your tendency to put things off. Developed by procrastination expert Piers Steel. http://bit.ly/procrastinate-test.

Tiny Habits program: This fun, free five-day online program is based on B. J. Fogg's research. Take it to get a jump start on implementing new habits into your life. http://tinyhabits.com.

The Pomodoro Technique: Find out more about this easy-to-implement strategy that enables you to get lots done in a very short period of time. http://pomodorotechnique.com.

FEATURED PRODUCTIVITY TOOLS

Below are the productivity tools mentioned in part 2. If they don't work on your device, it's easy to search for alternatives online.

RescueTime: Time management software that helps you understand your daily habits so you can focus and be more productive.

Freedom: Internet, social media, and app blocker to keep you distraction free while you're working.

SaneBox: Restores sanity to your in-box, filters important e-mails from the rest, handles auto-unsubscribes, sends e-mail reminders, and much more.

Unroll.me: Cleans up your in-box by combining subscriptions into a daily digest, plus offers a one-click unsubscribe function for unwanted newsletters.

Backdrop: A simple utility that fills your screen with a color/image so you can focus on the work that needs to get done.

f.lux: At night, reduces blue light emitted from your computer so it doesn't interfere with your ability to fall asleep.

Moment: Tracks smartphone/tablet usage automatically, even allowing you to set daily limits.

BreakFree: Controls smartphone addiction and helps you lead a healthy digital lifestyle.

Pocket: Saves interesting articles, videos, and more from the web for later viewing (on any of your devices).

Feedly: Aggregates your favorite news sites, blogs, YouTube channels, and RSS feeds in one place for easy reading/viewing.

Focus@Will: Neuroscience-based music subscription service that boosts concentration and focus.

Pomodoro One: Timer that jump-starts productivity and reminds you to take breaks.

I Done This: Helps you track and celebrate progress toward your goals.

Because this is an emerging field, some of these apps may disappear over time. I'm confident even better ones will replace them.

APPENDIX 3: BOOKS WORTH READING

These books helped me understand and master my time challenges. They offer lots of great insights, strategies, and ideas to help you be more successful at work and in life.

9 Things Successful People Do Differently, Heidi Grant Halvorson, Harvard Business Review, 2012.

18 Minutes: Find Your Focus, Master Distraction, and Get the Right Things Done, Peter Bregman, Business Plus, 2011.

168 Hours: You Have More Time than You Think, Laura Vanderkam, Portfolio, 2010.

Are You Fully Charged? The 3 Keys to Energizing Your Work and Life, Tom Rath, Silicon Guild, 2015.

Better than Before: Mastering the Habits of Our Everyday Lives, Gretchen Rubin, Crown, 2015.

Brain Rules: 12 Principles for Surviving and Thriving at Work, Home, and School, John Medina, Pear Press, 2008.

BrainChains: Discover Your Brain and Unleash Its Full Potential in a Hyperconnected, Multitasking World, Theo Compernolle, Compublications, 2014.

Counterclockwise: Mindful Health and the Power of Possibility, Ellen Langer, Ballantine Books, 2009.

Essentialism: The Disciplined Pursuit of Less, Greg McKeown, Crown Business, 2014.

Flow: The Psychology of Optimal Experience, Mihaly Csikszentmihalyi, Harper Perennial, 1990.

Four Seconds: All the Time You Need to Stop Counter-Productive Habits and Get the Results You Want, Peter Bregman, HarperOne, 2015.

Getting Things Done: The Art of Stress-Free Productivity, David Allen, Penguin, 2015.

I Know How She Does It: How Successful Women Make the Most of Their Time, Laura Vanderkam, Portfolio, 2015.

Mindfulness, Ellen Langer, Addison-Wesley, 1989.

Reality Is Broken: Why Games Make Us Better and How They Can Change the World, Jane McGonigal, Penguin, 2011.

Rethinking Positive Thinking: Inside the New Science of Motivation, Gabriele Oettingen, Current, 2014.

Smart Change: Five Tools to Create New and Sustainable Habits in Yourself and Others, Art Markman, Perigee, 2014.

The Achievement Habit: Stop Wishing, Start Doing, and Take Command of Your Life, Bernard Roth, HarperCollins, 2015.

The As If Principle: The Radically New Approach to Changing Your Life, Richard Wiseman, Simon and Schuster, 2014.

The ONE Thing: The Surprisingly Simple Truth behind Extraordinary Results, Gary Keller with Jay Papasan, Bard Press, 2012.

The Organized Mind: Thinking Straight in the Age of Information Overload, Daniel J. Levitin, Dutton, 2014.

The Power of Habit: Why We Do What We Do in Life and Business, Charles Duhigg, Random House, 2013.

The Power of Mindful Learning, Ellen J. Langer, Da Capo Press, 1997.

The Way We're Working Isn't Working: The Four Forgotten Needs That Energize Great Performance, Tony Schwartz, Free Press, 2010.

The Willpower Instinct: How Self-Control Works, Why It Matters, and What You Can Do to Get More of It, Kelly McGonigal, Avery, 2012.

Thinking, Fast and Slow, Daniel Kahneman, Farrar, Straus and Giroux, 2011.

Two Awesome Hours: Science-Based Strategies to Harness Your Best Time and Get Your Most Important Work Done, Josh Davis, HarperOne, 2015.

Willpower: Rediscovering the Greatest Human Strength, Roy F. Baumeister & John Tierney, Penguin, 2012.

Your Brain at Work: Strategies for Overcoming Distraction, Regaining Focus, and Working Smarter All Day Long, David Rock, HarperCollins, 2009.

ACKNOWLEDGMENTS

Writing a book is always a challenge. That's why I feel such a deep sense of gratitude for everything and everyone that made it all possible.

Most importantly, I appreciate my wonderful family. Fred, Katie, Ryan, Cynthia, and Cali—you kept me afloat as I struggled to conquer my own crazy busyness and then write about it. You are the most important people in my life; I value our relationships above all.

Believe it or not, I want to thank all my sales problems too. I hate them. They torture me. Until ultimately I turn them into challenges, which then motivates me to research, experiment, and find fresh strategies that were initially beyond my comprehension. Without these problems, my life would be boring.

To my sales-savvy colleagues, I'm so thankful for you. Every day you inspire me with the excellent body of work you contribute to our profession. I learn so much from you. Our conversations stimulate my thinking and enrich my life. I couldn't do this without your unwavering support.

I'm also eternally grateful for those really smart people in the world who don't love sales. Your keen minds and in-depth studies in fields like neuroscience, behavioral psychology, and cognitive sciences are fascinating. They fuel our future, helping us better understand our human instincts, how we think, what motivates us, and what frees us to do our best work—and lead our best life.

I give a heartfelt thanks to the people I work with every day: Natalie Horbachevsky, my incredible editor from Portfolio, who takes my writing to the next level; Katie Konrath, who makes sure my website and marketing are top-notch; and Chris Bedwell, who keeps me organized.

Finally, I thank *you*, the reader. Knowing that my work makes a difference gives me purpose—and that really matters.

NOTES

INTRODUCTION

2 **according to CSO Insights:** "Sales Enablement Optimization Study: 2015 Key Trends Analysis," CSO Insights, 2015, http://konrath.co/cso-insights.

CHAPTER 2: AGE OF DISTRACTION

17 **smartphone-carrying professionals (like salespeople):** Jennifer J. Deal, "Always On, Never Done? Don't Blame the Smartphone" (Center for Creative Leadership white paper, August 2013), http://bit.ly/ccl-whitepaper.

18 **John Pencavel, Stanford economist:** John Pencavel, "The Productivity of Working Hours" (discussion paper no. 8129, April 2014), http://ftp.iza.org/dp8129.pdf.

19 **author of *The Shallows*:** Nicholas Carr, *The Shallows: What the Internet Is Doing to Our Brains* (New York: W. W. Norton, 2011).

19 **recent Deloitte study:** "2015 Global Mobile Consumer Survey: US Edition," Deloitte.com, 2015, http://bit.ly/deloitte-mobile-survey.

19 **people check their phones:** Joanna Stern, "Cellphone Users Check Phones 150x/Day," ABC News, May 29, 2013, http://bit.ly/150xday.

20 **In *Hooked*:** Nir Eyal, *Hooked: How to Build Habit-Forming Products* (New York: Portfolio, 2014).

21 ***Driven to Distraction*:** Edward Hallowell and John Ratey, *Driven to Distraction* (New York: Anchor, 2011).

CHAPTER 3: TIME FOR A CHANGE

24 **actually a habit:** "Habits: Why We Do What We Do," *Harvard Business Review* interview with Charles Duhigg, June 2012, https://hbr.org/2012/06/habits-why-we-do-what-we-do.

24 **New Year's goals:** Sadie Dingfelder, "Solutions to Resolution Dilution," American Psychological Association, January 2004, http://apa.org/monitor/jan04/solutions.aspx.

25 **According to psychologist Art Markman:** Art Markman, *Smart Change: Five Tools to Create New and Sustainable Habits in Yourself and Others* (New York: Perigee, 2014).

25 **author of *Succeed*:** Heidi Grant Halvorson, *Succeed: How We Can Reach Our Goals* (New York: Plume, 2010).

26 **implementing "tiny habits":** B. J. Fogg, "Forget Big Change, Start with a Tiny Habit," TEDx Talk, 17:23, December 2012, http://bit.ly/tiny-tiny-habits.

CHAPTER 4: DISCOVER YOUR BASELINE

35 **the Hawthorne effect:** Kendra Cherry, "What Is the Hawthorne Effect?," *verywell*, 2015, http://bit.ly/hawthorne-study.

CHAPTER 5: E-MAIL: OUR BIGGEST NEMESIS

38 **joint study by UC Irvine:** Gloria J. Mark and Armand Cardello, "A Pace Not Dictated by Electrons: An Empirical Study of Work without Email," 2012, http://bit.ly/work-without-email.

39 **70 percent of e-mails received:** Judy Wajcman with Emily Rose,

"Constant Connectivity: Rethinking Interruptions at Work," *Organization Studies* 32, no. 7 (2011): 941–962.

39 **rats in the classic experiment:** Alfred K., "The Pleasure Center," April 2013, http://alfre.dk/the-pleasure-center.

40 **author of *Overload!*:** Jonathan Spira, *Overload! How Too Much Information Is Hazardous to Your Organization* (Hoboken: Wiley, 2011).

40 **person's recovery time:** "The Impact of Interruptions and Multitasking on Knowledge Worker Efficiency and Effectiveness," Basex, 2014, http://www.basexblog.com/2011/04/14/impact-multi.

CHAPTER 7: OVERCOME TIME-SUCKING TEMPTATIONS

46 **causes a mental logjam:** Kathrine Jebsen Moore, "How E-mail Harms Your Intelligence," *Bloomberg News*, accessed July 2016, http://bit.ly/mental-logjam.

46 **before being interrupted:** Clive Thompson, "Are You Checking Work E-mail in Bed? At the Dinner Table? On Vacation?," *Mother Jones*, May/June 2014, http://bit.ly/smartphone-addict.

CHAPTER 9: GET BACK ON TRACK

56 **Researchers at Columbia University found:** "Ever-So-Slight Delay Improves Decision-Making Accuracy," Columbia University Medical Center, March 7, 2014, http://bit.ly/postpone-decision

56 **According to Kelly McGonigal:** Kelly McGonigal, "The Willpower Instinct" video, Talks at Google, 54:02, January 2012, http://bit.ly/more-willpower.

57 **the WOOP method:** Gabriele Oettingen, *Rethinking Positive Thinking: Inside the New Science of Motivation* (New York: Current, 2014).

CHAPTER 10: TOTAL DIGITAL DECLUTTERING

59 **Princeton University discovered:** S. McMains and S. Kastner, "Interactions of Top-Down and Bottom-Up Mechanisms in Human Visual Cortex," *The Journal of Neuroscience* 32, no. 2 (January 2012): 587–97.

59 **messy digital environment:** M. Niemela and P. Saariluoma, "Layout Attributes and Recall," *Behaviour & Information Technology* 2, no. 5 (2003), http://bit.ly/digital-declutter.

62 **neuroscientist Daniel Levitin:** Daniel Levitin, "Why the Modern World Is Bad for Your Brain," *The Observer*, January 18, 2015, http://bit.ly/bad-for-brain.

CHAPTER 11: FIND YOUR FOCUS

68 **author of *Essentialism:*** Greg McKeown, *Essentialism: The Disciplined Pursuit of Less* (New York: Crown Business, 2014).

68 **In *The ONE Thing:*** Gary Keller, *The ONE Thing: The Surprisingly Simple Truth behind Extraordinary Results* (Austin: Bard Press, 2012).

70 **33 percent more time *with* customers:** Ryan Fuller, "What Makes Great Salespeople," *Harvard Business Review*, July 8, 2015, https://hbr.org/2015/07/what-makes-great-salespeople.

CHAPTER 12: THE CHOPPING BLOCK

72 **my to-do list of 150:** Roy F. Baumeister and John Tierney, *Willpower: Rediscovering the Great Human Strength* (New York: Penguin, 2012).

73 **According to a CSO Insights:** "Sales Management Optimization Study," CSO Insights, 2015, http://bit.ly/2015-sales-management.

74 **Forrester Research reports:** Mark Lindwall, "Why Don't Buyers Want to Meet with Your Salespeople?," Forrester Research, September 2014, http://bit.ly/unprepared-sellers.

75 **recommended by David Allen:** David Allen, *Getting Things Done: The Art of Stress-Free Productivity* (New York: Penguin, 2015).

CHAPTER 13: DESIGN A BETTER WAY

77 **"fog of distracted tinkering":** Cal Newport, "Deep Habits: Process Trumps Results for Daily Planning," *Study Hacks Blog*, August 14, 2015, http://bit.ly/distracted-tinkering.

78 **Tony Schwartz suggests:** Tony Schwartz, *The Way We're Working Isn't Working: The Four Forgotten Needs that Energize Great Performance* (New York: Free Press, 2010).

78 **American Psychological Association:** "Multitasking Switching Costs," American Psychological Association, March 20, 2006, http://www .apa.org/research/action/multitask.aspx.

80 **"map their territory":** Jeb Blount, *Fanatical Prospecting: The Ultimate Guide to Opening Sales Conversations and Filling the Pipeline by Leveraging Social Selling, Telephone, E-mail, Text, and Cold Calling* (Hoboken, NJ: Wiley, 2015).

81 **success rates go up 200 to 300 percent:** Heidi Grant Halvorson, "How to Make Yourself Do It When You Just Don't Want to: Three Strategies to Help You Stop Putting Things Off," *Psychology Today*, February 24, 2014, http://bit.ly/make-yourself-do-it.

CHAPTER 14: OPTIMIZE YOUR PLAN

84 **Jack Dorsey, CEO:** Kevin Kruse, "The Jack Dorsey Productivity Secret that Enables Him to Run Two Companies at Once," *Forbes*, October 12, 2015, http://bit.ly/jack-dorsey-secret.

CHAPTER 15: GIVE ME A BREAK

88 **study done by the Draugiem Group:** Julia Gifford, "The Rule of 52 and 17: It's Random but It Ups Your Productivity," *The Muse*, accessed July 2016, http://bit.ly/rule-of-52-17.

90 **Assume a power pose:** Amy Cuddy, "Your Body Language Shapes Who You Are," TED Talk, 21:02, June 2012, http://bit.ly/cuddy-TED -talk.

91 **added napping rooms:** Zoe Henry, "6 Companies (Including Uber) Where It's Okay to Nap," *Inc.*, September 2015, http://bit.ly/ok-to-nap.

91 **multiple Harvard studies:** "Napping May Not Be Such a No-No," *Harvard Health Publications*, Harvard Medical School, November 2009, http://bit.ly/30-minute-nap.

91 **morning breaks deliver:** "The Best Time of Day to Take a Break," *Washington Post*, September 14, 2015, http://bit.ly/take-break.

91 **"Sometimes, productivity science seems":** Derek Thompson, "A Formula for Perfect Productivity: Work for 52 Minutes, Break for 17," *The Atlantic*, September 17, 2014, http://konrath.co/justify-laziness.

CHAPTER 16: QUICK-START STRATEGIES

93 **Zeigarnik effect kicks in:** "Zeigarnik Effect: How Does the Zeigarnik Effect Affect Motivation?" *Wikiversity*, 2015, http://bit.ly/zeigarnik -effect.

95 **On these workers' self-described:** Teresa Amabile and Steven Kramer, "The Power of Small Wins," *Harvard Business Review*, May 2011, http://bit.ly/power-small-wins.

96 **"Overwhelm is a result":** Matthew Kimberley, "Overwhelm Begone—How to Be Underwhelmed," accessed July 2016, http://www.matthew kimberley.com/overwhelm.

CHAPTER 17: OPEN AND CLOSE STRONG

99 **high achievers have morning routines:** Laura Vanderkam, *What the Most Successful People Do before Breakfast* (New York: Portfolio, 2012).

99 **Dan Ariely, behavioral economist:** Eric Barker, "How to Be Efficient: Dan Ariely's 6 New Secrets to Managing Your Time," *Barking up the Wrong Tree*, 2015, http://bit.ly/be-efficient.

100 *Eat That Frog!:* Brian Tracy, *Eat That Frog! 21 Great Ways to Stop Procrastinating and Get More Done in Less Time* (San Francisco: Berrett-Koehler, 2007).

102 **reflecting for even a short time:** Gretchen Gavett, "The Power of Reflection at Work," *Harvard Business Review*, May 2014, http://bit .ly/reflect-at-work.

102 **Executive coach Chris Holmberg:** "The Most Dangerous Leadership Traps—and the 15-Minute Daily Practice that Will Save You," *First Round Review*, accessed July 2016, http://bit.ly/leadership-traps.

CHAPTER 18: THE TIME MASTER

107 **recent posting titled "Playing to Win":** Lydia Dishman, "Playing to Win: Could Gamification Boost Your Sales Success?," Yesware, accessed July 2016, http://www.yesware.com/blog/gamification.

109 **interview with Dr. Ellen Langer:** Ellen Langer with Krista Tippett, "Science of Mindlessness and Mindfulness," *On Being* podcast, September 10, 2015, http://bit.ly/langer-podcast.

CHAPTER 19: THE "AS IF" PHENOMENON

111 **he cites numerous studies:** Richard Wiseman, *The As If Principle: The Radically New Approach to Changing Your Life* (New York: Simon and Schuster, 2014).

111 **smiling instantly makes you happier:** Melinda Wenner, "Smile! It Could Make You Happier," *Scientific American*, September 1, 2009, http://bit.ly/smile-happier.

112 **father of cognitive clinical psychology:** George A. Kelly, *The Psychology of Personal Constructs, Volume One: Theory and Personality* (London: Routledge, 1991).

CHAPTER 21: GET INTO CHARACTER

121 **it takes about two weeks:** Richard Wiseman, *The As If Principle: The Radically New Approach to Changing Your Life* (New York: Simon and Schuster, 2014), 215–217.

CHAPTER 22: WORK WORTH DOING

127 **In his experiment:** "Putting a Face to a Name: The Art of Motivating Employees," Knowledge@Wharton, February 17, 2010, http://bit.ly/art-of-motivating.

CHAPTER 23: A REAL WAKE-UP CALL

131 **Huffington spoke about:** "INBOUND 2013: Arianna Huffington Keynote," YouTube video, 47:40, posted by HubSpot, August 21, 2013, http://bit.ly/success-sleep.

132 **In a Gallup study:** Jeffrey M. Jones, "In U.S., 40% Get Less than the Recommended Amount of Sleep," Gallup, December 19, 2013, http://bit.ly/more-sleep.

132 **669 middle-aged adults:** Diane Lauderdale, "New Study Shows People Sleep Even Less than They Think: Whites, Women and Wealthy Sleep Longer/Better," University of Chicago Medicine, July 3, 2006, http://bit.ly/new-sleep-study.

132 **don't get "enough" sleep:** Camille Peri, "What Lack of Sleep Does to Your Mind," WebMD, accessed July 2016, http://bit.ly/harder-to-concentrate.

CHAPTER 24: GET YOUR OOMPH BACK

137 **recent Wharton studies:** Cassie Mogilner, Zoe Chance, and Michael I. Norton, "Giving Time Gives You Time," Yale.edu, http://bit.ly/give-away-time.

137 **giving away time:** Cassie Mogilner, "You'll Feel Less Rushed if You Give Time Away," *Harvard Business Review*, September 2012, http://bit.ly/less-rushed.

138 **"thirty-seven percent better at sales":** Shawn Achor, "The Happy Secret to Better Work," TEDxBloomington, 12:20, May 2011, http://bit.ly/happiness-work.

138 **National Institute for Play:** Stuart Brown, *Play: How It Shapes the Brain, Opens the Imagination, and Invigorates the Soul* (New York: Avery, 2009).

CHAPTER 26: DO ABSOLUTELY NOTHING

145 **Harvard research shows:** John Tierney, "When the Mind Wanders, Happiness Also Strays," *New York Times*, November 15, 2010, http://bit.ly/lost-in-thought.

145 **people who practiced meditation:** David Levy, Jacob Wobbrock, Alred Kaszniak, and Marilyn Ostergren, "The Effects of Mindfulness Meditation Training on Multitasking in a High-Stress Information Environment," University of Washington, 2012, http://bit.ly/less-distracted.

146 **more flexible in their thinking:** Kimberly Schaufenbuel, "Bringing Mindfulness to the Workplace," UNC Executive Development, 2014, http://bit.ly/mindfulness-in-workplace.

148 **free five-day e-mail course:** Stanford professor B. J. Fogg's online workshop: http://tinyhabits.com/join/.

148 **"most important productivity tool":** Jeff Weiner, "The Importance of Scheduling Nothing," *LinkedIn Pulse*, April 3, 2013, http://bit.ly/weiner-do-nothing.

CHAPTER 27: WALKING IS WORK

151 **According to John Medina:** John Medina, *Brain Rules: 12 Principles for Surviving and Thriving at Work, Home, and School* (Seattle: Pear Press, 2008).

151 **average office worker sits:** Rory Heath, "Sitting Ducks—Sedentary Behavior and Its Health Risks," *British Journal of Sports Medicine Blog*, January 21, 2015, http://bit.ly/too-much-sitting.

151 **moving for at least two hours:** "The Sedentary Office: A Growing Case for Change towards Better Health and Productivity," *British Journal of Sports Medicine*, press release, June 2, 2015, http://bit.ly/sedentary-office.

151 **a person's creativity increased:** Marily Oppezzo and Daniel L. Schwartz, "Give Your Ideas Some Legs: The Positive Effect of Walking on Creative Thinking," *Journal of Experimental Psychology* 40, no. 4 (2014): 1142–1152, http://bit.ly/walking-creativity.

152 **"sitting has become the smoking":** "Got a Meeting? Take a Walk." Nilofer Merchant, TED Talk, 3:28, February 2013, http://bit.ly/walk-walk.

CHAPTER 28: SET UP FOR SUCCESS

155 **"cones of silence":** "6 CEO Productivity Tips," *CityLife*, September 8, 2015, http://bit.ly/ceo-productivity-tips.

156 **productivity was boosted by up to 35 percent:** "Office Plants Boost Well-Being at Work," University of Exeter, July 9, 2013, http://bit.ly/worker-productivity.

157 **9 percent more productive:** Mary Czerwinski, Greg Smith, Tim Regan, Brian Meyers, George Robertson, and Gary Starkweather, "Toward Characterizing the Productivity Benefits of Very Large Displays," Microsoft Research, January 1, 2003, http://bit.ly/larger-screens.

CHAPTER 29: TAP INTO TRIGGERS

162 **create a viable vision:** Mark Lindwall, "To Win against Increasing Competition, Equip Your Salespeople with a Deeper Understanding of Your Buyers," Forrester Research, January 27, 2014, http://bit.ly/viable-vision.

164 **65 percent of best-in-class firms:** "Trigger Events: Making the Most of Real-Time Sales Intelligence," Aberdeen Group, February 2014, http://bit.ly/research-triggers.

CHAPTER 30: DEVELOP TIME-SAVING SYSTEMS

166 **eight to twelve attempts:** "Sales Tips and Tricks—How Many Contact Attempts?," InsideSales.com, accessed July 2016 http://www.insidesales.com/tips/number-of-contact-attempts/.

170 **people are four times more likely to buy:** Scott Tousley, "107 Mind-Blowing Sales Statistics that Will Help You Sell Smarter," HubSpot, September 14, 2015, http://bit.ly/107-sales-stats.

CHAPTER 31: UNCLOG YOUR PIPELINE

174 **according to research from CEB:** Karl Schmidt, Brent Adamson, and Anna Bird, "Making the Consensus Sale," *Harvard Business Review*, March 2015, https://hbr.org/2015/03/making-the-consensus-sale.

CHAPTER 33: MAKE DECISIONS SIMPLER

183 **change initiatives are abandoned:** Patrick Spenner and Karl Schmidt, "Two Numbers You Should Care About," CEB, March 31, 2015, http://bit.ly/ceb-two-numbers.

APPENDIX 1: LEADING A HIGHLY PRODUCTIVE SALES TEAM

201 **Research by Pace Productivity:** Mark Ellwood, "How Sales Reps Spend Their Time," Pace Productivity, accessed July 2016, http://bit.ly/sales-productivity-report.

201 **VoloMetrix reports that top sellers:** Ryan Fuller, "What Makes Great Salespeople," *Harvard Business Review*, July 8, 2015, https://hbr.org/2015/07/what-makes-great-salespeople.

INDEX

accelerating sales, 159–60, 170,
    177–78
  for sales teams, 205–6
  triggers and, 162–63, 165
account targeting, 159, 161–62,
    166–71
Achor, Shawn, 138
Adamson, Brent, 140
Agile Selling (Konrath),
    3, 171
Ariely, Dan, 99
"as if" strategy, 110–14, 180
  avatars in, 117, 120–21
  duration of, 113, 117–18, 121
  as fun, 116, 121
  Time Master and, 110, 113,
    116–17, 119
  transformational experiments
    on, 105, 110, 117–18,
    120–21

Backdrop, 47, 54, 63
baselines, 33–37
bigger clients, 159, 187–91, 193
  expectations of, 189–90
  researching for, 189–91
  revenue ladder and,
    188–90
  systematizing and, 170
blind spots, 176, 192
Blount, Jeb, 80
BreakFree, 37, 62
breaks, 49, 52–53, 58, 63, 78, 88–92,
    104, 204
  quick-start strategies and,
    95, 97
  Time Master and, 109, 122
  work environments and, 154

Carr, Nicholas, 19
CEB, 140, 174, 183

challenges, 3–4, 6–7, 27, 70, 85,
    120, 126, 137, 187, 200
  bigger clients and, 170, 189–90
  distractions and, 20, 31, 51
  help and, 142–43
  pipelines and, 173
  quick-start strategies and, 93, 97
  sales teams and, 3, 201, 203,
    205, 207
  simplifying and, 183, 185
  sleep and, 132, 134
  Time Master and, 109, 113, 122
  triggers and, 164–65
  upward spiral and,
    180–82, 192
  walking and, 152
change, 18, 23–28, 57, 87, 97–98,
    102, 128, 134, 171, 187,
    198–200, 202
  "as if" strategy and, 111,
    116–17, 121
  crazy busyness and, 23–24,
    28, 198
  e-mail and, 23, 25, 40
  failures and, 24–26, 28
  final thoughts on, 199–200
  habits and, 23–26, 30, 200
  help and, 140, 143
  mindfulness and, 146–47
  pipelines and, 73, 172–75
  scheduling and, 81, 100
  simplifying and, 183–86
  steps in, 25–28, 30
  Time Master and, 108, 115–17
  time tracking and, 33, 35–37

  triggers and, 161–63, 165, 192
  upward spiral and, 178–81
  work environments and, 154, 158
Cirillo, Francesco, 94
competition, 3, 85, 94, 107, 128,
    143, 150, 159, 170, 179, 200
  simplifying and, 185–86
  spare time activities and, 136, 138
  time tracking and, 35–36
  triggers and, 161–62
crazy busyness, 1, 3–4, 9–16, 29,
    36, 114, 125
  changing and, 23–24, 28, 198
  distractions and, 12–13, 21,
    198–99
  kissing it good-bye, 198–99
  of Konrath's day, 11–15, 197–98
  simplifying and, 159, 183, 186
  Time Master and, 113, 115, 122
Crispo, Juliana, 83–84
CSO Insights, 2, 73
curiosity, 3, 130, 167, 177, 184, 190,
    199, 205
  help and, 143–44
  upward spiral and, 179,
    181–82, 192
customer relationship
    management (CRM), 1, 16,
    60, 69, 73, 79–80, 144, 176,
    181, 206

decision making, 3, 34, 56–59, 96,
    100, 112, 140, 158, 171, 189, 197
  breaks and, 89–90
  changing and, 23–24, 27

crazy busyness and, 12–13,
159, 199
distractions and, 21, 51–52
e-mail and, 42–45
focus and, 67–68, 70
and getting back on track,
56–57
mindfulness and, 146, 148
pipelines and, 73, 103, 172, 174,
176–77
planning and, 85–87, 104
scheduling and, 81–82, 85
simplifying and, 183–86, 193
sleep and, 131–32
Time Master and, 108, 116
triggers and, 161–62, 165, 176
upward spiral and, 179, 181
on what you won't do, 86–87, 104
digital decluttering, 59–61, 63
distractions, 4, 6, 15–26, 29–31, 35,
51–59, 61–65, 91, 103, 105,
120, 125, 132, 145, 150, 159,
168, 197–99
brain in, 18–24, 29
changing and, 23, 25–26
crazy busyness and, 12–13, 21,
198–99
digital decluttering and, 59, 61, 63
eliminating of, 51–55, 59
e-mail and, 17, 19–22, 31, 38–39,
52–53, 55
and getting back on track, 56–58
planning and, 74, 101
productivity and, 15–19, 51, 53, 62
sales teams and, 201–2, 206

scheduling and, 49, 54, 77, 81
temptations and, 20, 47–49, 51, 54
Time Master and, 22, 108, 113,
115, 119, 123
work environments and, 22, 29,
154, 156, 158
doing nothing, 145–49
Dorsey, Jack, 84
Draugiem Group, 88
Duhigg, Charles, 24

e-mail, 5–6, 9, 16, 34–49, 60, 133,
146, 148, 179, 197
bigger clients and, 189–90
breaks and, 89, 92
changing and, 23, 25, 40
in crazy-busy day, 12, 14–15
distractions and, 17, 19–22, 31,
38–39, 52–53, 55
electronic notifications on,
42, 45, 62
flexibility on, 40–42
help and, 140, 144
nonessential, 43–44, 63
sales teams and, 202, 204, 206
scheduling and, 43, 45, 62, 79,
85, 104
systematizing and, 166–69
temptations and, 43, 47–49
time limits on, 52, 55, 62–63
Time Master and, 108–9
time tracking and, 34–37
triggers and, 42, 164
walking and, 150–51
weaning from, 42–43

e-mail (*cont.*)
    work environments and, 156–57
    work worth doing and, 127, 129
Emerson, Melinda, 84
energy, 75, 86, 95, 131, 136–39, 141
    breaks and, 90, 122
    mindfulness and, 146–47
    play and, 137–38
    positiveness and, 125, 138
    Time Master and, 109, 122
ExecVision.io, 205
exercising, 88, 90, 95, 199

Facebook, 15, 35, 37, 40, 46, 49, 89,
    167, 170
feedback, 143, 180–81, 205
Feedly, 49, 63
focus, 14, 65, 67–71, 74, 76, 133,
    138, 140, 152, 157, 162, 169,
    178, 185, 189, 198
    breaks and, 88, 90, 95
    changing and, 23, 25
    distractions and, 16–17, 19, 21,
        52–53, 54
    and getting back on track, 56, 63
    mindfulness and, 145–48
    and opening and closing strong,
        100, 102
    pipelines and, 73, 173, 177, 192
    planning and, 84, 86–87
    priorities and, 68–71, 88, 103
    quick-start strategies and, 95, 97
    sales teams and, 202–5, 207
    temptations and, 48–49
    Time Master and, 109, 113

Fogg, B. J., 26, 148–49
Forrester Research, 74, 162
Freedom, 48, 50, 53–55, 58, 60, 63
Fuller, Ryan, 70

getting back on track, 56–58, 63
goals, 4–5, 9–10, 17, 70, 72, 95, 100,
    127, 138, 190, 198
    changing and, 24–28
    and getting back on track,
        57–58
    help and, 140–41
    planning and, 81, 84, 86
    scheduling and, 78, 81
    Time Master and, 108, 122
    time tracking and, 34–37
    upward spiral and, 178, 180–81
Grant, Adam, 127–28
gratification, 19, 48
Gsell, Carolyn, 146–47

habits, 6, 47, 105, 151, 202
    changing and, 9, 23–26, 30, 200
    e-mail and, 39, 42
    and opening and closing strong,
        99, 102
    sleep and, 132, 134
    Time Master and, 116–17
Halvorson, Heidi Grant, 25, 81
Hearl, Russ, 83
help, 140–44, 164, 185
    asking for, 141–44
    bigger clients and, 190–91
    with internal roadblocks,
        141–42

sales teams and, 201–3, 205
    when strategically stumped,
        142–43
Holmberg, Chris, 102
HubSpot, 131, 144, 206
Huffington, Arianna, 131–32
Hunter, Emily, 91

InsideSales.com, 166
interruptions, 16, 46, 63, 197
    distractions and, 19, 54
    e-mail and, 40, 43
    planning and, 85–86
    quick-start strategies and,
        93–94
    sales teams and, 204
    scheduling and, 81–82
    temptations and, 47–50
    work environments and,
        154–55, 158

Keller, Gary, 68, 71, 103
Kelly, George, 112–13, 121
Kosakowski, Jack, 69

Langer, Ellen, 109–10
LinkedIn, 17, 40, 48, 60, 93,
        109, 144–45, 148, 174, 190,
        197, 206
    in crazy-busy day, 13, 15
    and getting back on track, 57–58
    systematizing and, 166–70
    time tracking and, 35–36
    work environments and, 156–57
London, Jonathan, 147

Media Junction, 128–29
meditation, 145–48
Medtronic, 128
Meeker, Mary, 19
Merchant, Nilofer, 152
mindfulness, 145–49
Moment, 36–37, 62

Norcross, John, 24

Oettingen, Gabriele, 57–58
ONE Thing, the, 68–71, 76, 78, 97,
        103, 109
opening and closing strong,
        98–102, 104
Oppezzo, Marily, 151–52

Pace Productivity, 201
Pencavel, John, 18
phones, 27, 29, 53, 62, 144, 146
    bigger clients and, 189–90
    in crazy-busy day, 12, 14
    digital decluttering and,
        59–60, 63
    distractions and, 16–17, 19
    e-mail and, 42
    sales teams and, 204
    systematizing and, 168
    temptations and, 46–48
    time tracking and, 35–37
    triggers and, 164
pipelines:
    correct contacts in, 174–75
    misjudged interest in, 175
    planning and, 84, 87, 176

pipelines (*cont.*)
  prospects and, 4, 69, 72–73, 78, 103, 172–77
  and reasons to continue, 175–76
  unclogging of, 172–77, 192
  why deals get stuck and, 173–76
planning, 53, 65, 73–74, 90, 98, 109, 114, 134, 147, 158, 185, 190
  changing and, 24–28
  color-coded calendaring in, 83–84, 104
  distractions and, 74, 101
  and getting back on track, 56–58
  less time in, 85–86
  optimizing in, 83–87
  pipelines and, 84, 87, 176
  quick-start strategies and, 94–97
  rule creation and, 87, 104
  scheduling and, 77–81, 83–86
  systematizing and, 169, 192
  thematic, 84–85, 87, 104–5
  what you won't do and, 86–87
play, 12, 15, 20, 61, 120, 133
  breaks and, 88, 91
  energy and, 137–38
  planning and, 86–87
  Time Master and, 107–8, 113
Pomodoro Technique, 94–97, 104
positiveness, 90, 115, 127
  changing and, 25–26
  energy and, 125, 138
power hours, 203–4

priorities, 4–7, 52, 65, 100, 122, 190, 204
  digital decluttering and, 60–61
  focus and, 68–71, 88, 103
  pipelines and, 173–74, 192
  scheduling and, 77–78
  triggers and, 161–64
problems, 2–5, 7, 14, 18, 33, 58, 61, 101, 135–36, 138, 159, 172, 185, 187, 206
  "as if" strategy and, 112, 121
  help and, 141–42, 144
  upward spiral and, 180, 182, 192
  walking and, 150, 152
productivity, 2–7, 11, 29, 65, 74, 76, 87, 126
  "as if" strategy and, 105, 114, 117, 120
  breaks and, 88, 91–92
  challenges and, 3–4
  changing and, 23, 30
  crazy busyness and, 198–99
  distractions and, 15–19, 51, 53, 62
  e-mail and, 40, 42, 45
  focus and, 68
  and getting back on track, 57–58
  help and, 140, 144
  mindfulness and, 145, 148
  and opening and closing strong, 99, 101–2
  quick-start strategies and, 93, 95
  sales teams and, 201–7
  scheduling and, 77–79, 81–82, 104
  sleep and, 131–35

spare time activities and, 137
systematizing and, 167–69
temptations and, 49
Time Master and, 107, 113,
  115–17
time tracking and, 33–34, 37
triggers and, 162
walking and, 153
work environments and, 154–58
work worth doing and, 127–29
proposals, 9, 14, 16, 33–34, 39, 54,
  65, 129, 151, 155
  sales teams and, 204–5
  scheduling and, 78–79, 81, 85
  systematizing and, 170, 192
prospects, 9, 31, 65, 75–76, 100, 197
  "as if" strategy and, 111–12
  bigger clients and, 170,
    189–90, 193
  crazy busyness and, 12–14, 159,
    183, 186
  distractions and, 22, 54
  e-mail and, 38–39
  focus and, 67, 69
  mindfulness and, 147
  pipelines and, 4, 69, 72–73, 78,
    103, 172–77
  planning and, 84, 87, 96–97
  quick-start strategies and, 94,
    96–97
  sales teams and, 206
  scheduling and, 78–81
  simplifying and, 159, 183–86, 193
  systematizing and, 166–67,
    170–71, 192

triggers and, 161–62, 165
upward spiral and, 178–81
walking and, 150
work worth doing and, 127–29

quick-start strategies, 93–97
  Pomodoro Technique and,
    94–97, 104
  for supersized projects, 96–97

Rath, Tom, 129
Reni, Jake, 157–58
RescueTime, 34–37, 62, 203
rewards, 12, 39, 55
  breaks and, 90
  distractions and, 18–20
  temptations and, 48–49
  Time Master and, 108
Rimini Street, 128
rules, 43, 57, 63, 87, 104, 204

sales, selling:
  quotas in, 1–2, 31, 70, 89, 159, 178
  statistics on, 2, 12, 70, 73–74,
    162, 166, 201
sales teams, 2–3, 7, 69, 128, 157, 168
  accelerating sales for, 205–6
  challenges and, 3, 201, 203,
    205, 207
  in crazy-busy day, 13
  expanding knowledge base of,
    202–3
  leading highly productive, 201–7
  role models for, 206
  rules for, 204

sales teams (*cont.*)
    time protectors for, 203–4
    upward spiral for, 205
SaneBox, 43, 55, 63
scheduling, 6, 27, 63, 76–86,
    103–4, 158, 165
    in blocks of time, 78, 104, 109,
      122, 139
    buffers in, 79–80, 104
    crazy busyness and, 183
    distractions and, 49, 54, 77, 81
    e-mail and, 43, 45, 62, 79,
      85, 104
    energy and, 139
    geography-based, 80
    grouping similar activities in,
      78–79
    and opening and closing strong,
      100–101
    planning and, 77–81, 83–86
    positiveness and, 138
    of quitting times, 80–82
    sales teams and, 204–5
    simplifying and, 183
    sleep and, 133
    systematizing and, 168–69
    temptations and, 47, 49
    Time Master and, 109, 122
Schwartz, Daniel, 151–52
Schwartz, Tony, 78
Selling to Big Companies
    (Konrath), 3, 189
simplicity, 121, 159, 183–86
    creating tools in, 185–86, 193
    road maps in, 184, 193

starting smaller in, 185
talking about tough stuff in,
    184–85, 193
Time Master and, 116
sleep, 3–4, 39, 91, 125, 131–35,
    147, 199
SNAP Selling (Konrath), 3, 140,
    171, 186
socializing, 88, 90–92, 101, 199
social media, 16, 31, 49, 60, 69, 89,
    167, 170, 197
spare time activities, 136–39
Spira, Jonathan, 40
stress, 19, 49, 54, 61, 125
    breaks and, 88–90
    e-mail and, 43
    help and, 141
    pipelines and, 176
    quick-start strategies and, 93
supersized projects, 96–97
systematizing, 24, 77, 81
    time-saving and, 166–71, 192

temptations, 46–51
    "as if" strategy and, 111
    changing and, 25
    crazy busyness and, 199
    distractions and, 20, 47–49, 51, 54
    e-mail and, 43, 47–49
thinking, 46–47, 58, 61, 63, 98–101,
    126, 144, 159, 199–201
    "as if" strategy and, 111–12,
      114, 121
    breaks and, 88–91, 95
    changing and, 23–25, 27

digital decluttering and, 59
distractions and, 18–24, 29, 31,
    52–53, 62
e-mail and, 39–40, 42–44
focus and, 67, 70
help and, 141
mindfulness and, 147, 149
and opening and closing strong,
    99–101
pipelines and, 172, 175–76
planning and, 74, 86–87
quality of, 4–6, 62, 94
quick-start strategies and,
    93–94
sales teams and, 201, 204–5
scheduling and, 77, 79–81, 104
sleep and, 131–35
systematizing and, 167,
    170–71, 192
temptations and, 49
Time Master and, 119
triggers and, 161, 163
walking and, 150–52
work environments and,
    155–58
Thompson, Derek, 91
Thoreau, Henry David, 65
time:
    blocks of, 78, 104, 109, 122, 139
    not having enough, 1–2, 27, 85
    optimizing and maximizing of,
        65–66, 103
    recovering lost, 7, 32, 62–64
    saving, 6, 166–71, 192
    tracking of, 33–37, 62, 88

Time Master, 105–10, 200
    "as if" strategy and, 110, 113,
        116–17, 119
    distractions and, 22, 108, 113,
        115, 119, 123
    duration of, 116–17
    Manifesto, 106, 119–20, 122–23
    why it worked, 115–17
Toman, Nick, 140
triggers, 192
    bigger clients and, 170
    distractions and, 20, 63
    e-mail and, 42, 164
    identifying of, 162–63
    keeping updated on, 163–64
    mindfulness and, 148–49
    pipelines and, 173, 176
    play and, 138
    systematizing and, 170
    tapping into, 161–65
    temptations and, 49
    use of, 164–65
Twain, Mark, 100
Twitter, 15, 48, 84, 167, 170, 197

Unroll.me, 44, 55, 63
upward spiral:
    challenges in, 180–82, 192
    creating of, 178–82, 192
    curiosity and, 179, 181–82, 192
    feedback and, 180–81
    getting smarter and, 179–82, 192
    for sales teams, 205
urgency, 41, 43, 48, 68–70, 94,
    155, 173

value, 1, 4–5, 9, 44, 95, 97, 102,
    187–88, 199
  digital decluttering and, 59
  distractions and, 20
  help and, 141, 143–44
  of mindfulness, 145–46
  pipelines and, 73, 172–73, 175
  planning and, 74
  sales teams and, 202
  scheduling and, 80
  simplifying and, 184
  of time, 20, 31, 80, 109, 122, 202
  Time Master and, 109, 119, 122
  upward spiral and, 179–81
  walking and, 151
  work worth doing and, 129–30
Vanderkam, Laura, 99
VoloMetrix, 70, 201
volunteer work, 81, 136–37, 139

Wajcman, Judy, 39
walking, 58, 109–10, 133,
    150–53
  breaks and, 88, 90, 95
Weiner, Jeff, 145, 148
Wilson, Glenn, 46
Wiseman, Richard, 111
WOOP method, 57–58, 63
work environments, 90, 143,
    153–58
  digital decluttering and,
    60–61
  distractions and, 22, 29, 154,
    156, 158
  interruptions in, 154–55, 158
  optimizing of, 154–58
  reorganizing of, 155–56
  rethinking of digital,
    156–58

BRING
MORE SALES,
LESS TIME
TO YOUR SALE
CONFERENCE

Jill Konrath's keynote will inspire your group to work smarter and drive more revenue.

With her passionate delivery, fresh strategies, and highly engaging style, she's always a top-rated speaker.

You'll get education, entertainment, and motivation—all in one bundle. Customized for your people.

For more information, visit jillkonrath.com